Are you interested in

a course management system that would

save you time & effort?

If the answer is *yes*, **CourseCompass is for you.**

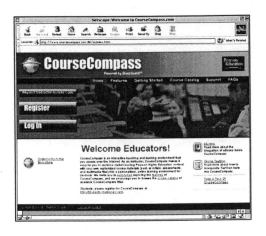

Instructor's Manual and Test Bank

for

Spradley and McCurdy

Conformity and Conflict
Readings in Cultural Anthropology

Eleventh Edition

prepared by

David W. McCurdy
Macalester College

Boston   New York   San Francisco
Mexico City   Montreal   Toronto   London   Madrid   Munich   Paris
Hong Kong   Singapore   Tokyo   Cape Town   Sydney

To obtain permission(s) to use the material from this work, please submit a written request to Allyn and Bacon, Permissions Department, 75 Arlington Street, Boston, MA 02116 or fax your request to 617-848-7320.

ISBN 0-205-37252-X

Printed in the United States of America

10 9 8 7 6 5 4 3 2 1   08 07 06 05 04 03 02

PREFACE

This supplement has been developed especially for use with the Eleventh Edition of *Conformity and Conflict: Readings in Cultural Anthropology*. Included are summaries of each article, true or false questions, and multiple choice questions. Answers for true or false questions are indicated by the inclusion of a T or F before each question. The correct answer for each multiple choice question is marked by an asterisk.

The addition of key concepts to *Conformity and Conflict* starting with the sixth edition has permitted an expansion of the number and scope of questions about each article. Questions are largely confined to the main ideas and facts presented in each article, but there are also some questions written to test the relationship of key concepts with articles.

You may use the questions included in this supplement in at least three ways: in their present form, in a form altered to meet your requirements, and as a source of ideas for new questions. You may prefer to rewrite questions to fit your style, course content, and students. Most instructors use the selections in *Conformity and Conflict* to illustrate course concepts and theory. It is often possible to work material from lectures, a text, or other sources into the framework of questions included in this manual.

Finally, you may want to use the questions presented here as a source of ideas for new questions. It may be possible to ask something using a simpler and clearer question frame. Ideas for new question topics often emerge from a review of old test items. However you decide to use them, I hope that the article summaries, concept definitions, and questions presented here will be helpful to you.

David McCurdy

CONTENTS

Instructor's Manual and Test Bank

for

Spradley and McCurdy

Conformity and Conflict
Readings in Cultural Anthropology

Eleventh Edition

PART 1

CULTURE AND ETHNOGRAPHY

The introduction to Part 1 discusses the concept of culture and the nature of ethnographic fieldwork with special emphasis on the following definitions.

KEY DEFINITIONS

Culture is the acquired (learned) knowledge that people use to generate behavior and interpret experience.

Ethnography is the process of discovering and describing a particular culture.

A **microculture** is a system of cultural knowledge characteristic of a subgroup within a larger society.

Tacit culture is culture that is not coded in language by a people, such as speaking distances.

Explicit culture is culture that people are consciously aware of and can talk about.

An **informant** is an individual from whom anthropologists learn a culture.

A **respondent** is an individual who responds to survey questions normally associated with survey research.

A **subject** is a person who is observed by social scientists conducting experimental social or psychological research.

Naive realism is the belief that people everywhere see the world in the same way.

Ethnocentrism is the belief and feeling that one's own culture is best.

Culture shock is a state of anxiety that results from cross-cultural misunderstanding.

Detached observation is a research approach in which investigators observe human behavior and create their own categories and theories to describe and explain it.

QUESTIONS

True or False ?

F 1. Culture is the patterned behavior characteristic of a group of people.

T 2. Detached observation is a research approach in which investigators observe human behavior and create their own categories and theories to describe and explain it.

F 3. A microculture is the patterned behavior characteristic of a subgroup within a larger society.

T 4. An informant is what anthropologists call the individuals from whom they learn a culture.

F 5. Tacit culture is cultural knowledge that informants consciously hide from the anthropologist during field work.

Multiple Choice

1. Sir Edward Burnett Tylor is known for his early definition of
    a. ethnography.
    * b. culture.
    c. naive realism.
    d. culture shock.
    e. detached observation.

2. When they do ethnographic fieldwork, anthropologists interview
    a. respondents.
    b. subjects.
    * c. informants.
    d. participants.
    e. objects.

3. The process of discovering and describing a particular culture is called
    a. interviewing.
    b. ethnology.
    c. participant observation.
    * d. ethnography.
    e. ethnocentrism.

4. The view that all people see and understand the world in the same way is called
   * a. naive realism.
     b. culture shock.
     c. ethnocentrism.
     d. arbitrariness.
     e. detached observation.

5. The belief and feeling that one's own culture is best is called
     a. culture shock.
     b. cultural relativism.
     c. naive realism.
     d. detached observation.
   * e. ethnocentrism.

Article 1

Ethnography and Culture   JAMES P. SPRADLEY

Summary In this introductory chapter from his book, *Participant Observation*, Spradley defines and emphasizes the importance of ethnographic fieldwork and the concept of culture. Ethnography is the work of describing a culture. It requires the discovery of the native's or insider's point of view. Cultural behavior consists of the actions generated by cultural knowledge. Cultural artifacts, based on cultural behavior and cultural knowledge, are the things people make or shape from natural resources. Culture, itself, is the socially acquired knowledge that people use to generate behavior and interpret experience. Different cross-cultural interpretations of the same event easily cause misunderstandings. Culture may also be explicit (part of our conscious awareness) or tacit (outside awareness). The meaning of things for members of a group is at the heart of the culture concept, a point related to Blumer's notion of symbolic interaction. Spradley concludes by characterizing culture as a map, a guide to action and interpretation.

QUESTIONS

True or False?

F   1.   Spradley defines culture as behavior, artifacts, and knowledge.

T   2.   Anthropologists, such as George Hicks, look for inside meaning when they do ethnographic research.

F   3.   Tacit culture refers to cultural knowledge that informants consciously hide from the ethnographer.

T   4.   Herbert Blumer developed a theory of symbolic interaction.

F   5.   The concept of "explicit culture" is a key part of Herbert Blumer's theory of symbolic interaction.

T   6.   Spradley argues that culture is more like a map, guiding human action, rather than a strict set of rules requiring specific behavior.

Multiple Choice

1. According to Spradley, the term "ethnography" refers to
    a.   cross-cultural explanation.
    * b.   the discovery and description of the culture of a particular group.
    c.   the statistical testing of hypotheses in the field, using survey questionnaires.
    d.   the discovery of ethnic subgroups within complex societies.
    e.   the process of cross-cultural classification, comparison, and explanation.

2. According to Spradley, culture, itself, is a kind of
    a.   behavior.
    b.   artifact.
    * c.   knowledge.
    d.   symbolic interaction.
    e.   ideal system.

3. According to Spradley, the belief that people everywhere interpret the world in the same way is called
    * a.   naive realism.
    b.   ethnography.
    c.   cultural behavior.
    d.   explicit culture.
    e.   tacit culture.

4. Which of the following is the best example of an action based on a tacit cultural rule for members of U.S. society?
    a.   chewing with one's mouth closed
    b.   driving on the right side of the street
    c.   giving your father "his" chair in front of the family television
    * d.   moving to the opposite side of an elevator when there is only one other person in it
    e.   formatting a business letter

5. The idea that human beings act toward things on the basis of the meanings they have for them is a tenet of
    a.   naive realism.
    b.   explicit culture.
    c.   tacit culture.
    d.   ethnographic research techniques.
    * e.   symbolic interaction.

6. According to Spradley, the actions generated by cultural knowledge are called
   a.   social control.
* b.   cultural behavior.
   c.   cultural generation.
   d.   cultural artifacts.
   e.   explicit culture.

Article 2

Eating Christmas in the Kalahari   RICHARD BORSHAY LEE

Summary   In this article, Lee describes a classic case of cross-cultural misunderstanding that occurred near the completion of his fieldwork among the !Kung Bushmen. To thank the !Kung for allowing him to live and work among them, Lee decided to donate an especially large ox for them to eat at their annual Christmas feast. To his dismay, the !Kung seemed disappointed with the animal he had chosen, claiming that it was too thin, old, and sick. Their attitude persisted even after the butchered ox proved to be so large and fat that it fed 150 people for two days.

Only later did Lee discover that the !Kung customarily denigrate and ridicule hunters who have killed large game in order to "cool" their potential arrogance. To Lee, the ox meant a gift, and in American culture gifts should be reciprocated with thanks and appreciation. To the !Kung, the ox was a large animal to be shared, something hunters contribute regularly. For them, the provider must be kept in line lest he become impressed by his own importance (a position related to the !Kung value on equality). Because of these different cultural interpretations of the same act, cross-cultural misunderstanding resulted.

As a postscript to this article, remember that the !Kung were studied by Lee in the 60s; few live as foragers today. For an update on the !Kung see the epilogue to article 11 by Lee and Biesele.

QUESTIONS

True or False?

F 1. !Kung ridiculed the ox Lee gave them for their Christmas feast because the animal was too thin and old.

F 2. Lee's gift of a Christmas ox was ridiculed by the !Kung because he misunderstood their criteria for a desirable animal.

T 3. The !Kung ridiculed the ox given them by Lee for their Christmas feast because this is the usual way they "cool" the arrogance of people who provide important things for others.

T 4. The !Kung regularly understate their own hunting achievements to avoid looking arrogant.

F 5. !Kung regularly express admiration for one another's hunting achievements.

T 6. The misunderstanding that Lee experienced with the !Kung was based on different cultural meanings for Lee's gift of a Christmas ox.

Multiple Choice

1. !Kung expressed disappointment with the ox Lee gave them for the Christmas feast because
   a. the animal was too thin and old.
   * b. this was their way to "cool" a giver's potential arrogance.
   c. the animal came from on outsider.
   d. they were afraid that Lee would take the animal back if they showed approval.
   e. they were angry at Lee for intruding on their lives.

2. The cross-cultural misunderstanding experienced between Lee and the !Kung occurred over
   * a. the cultural meaning of the gift of an ox.
   b. the criteria for defining what makes an ox desirable.
   c. the way Lee gave them the ox.
   d. the cultural meaning of oxen.
   e. the poor condition of the ox.

3. According to Lee, a !Kung hunter
   a. eats all of a kill himself.
   b. shares game only with his own family.
   c. gives all the meat from an animal he has killed to the man who made the arrow he used.
   * d. shares what he kills with others and expects them to reciprocate.
   e. may do anything he likes with an animal he kills.

4. According to Lee, when a !Kung hunter kills a large animal, he is likely to tell others
   a. "I have killed a large giraffe."
   b. "I have killed a big one in the bush."
   * c. "I am no good for hunting. I just saw a little tiny one."
   d. "A giraffe happened to step in front of my flying arrow."
   e. "Come help me carry. There is much heavy meat."

5. The way the !Kung treated Richard Lee's gift of a Christmas ox reveals their value on
   a. individualism.
   b. male dominance.
   c. family solidarity.
   d. identification with nature.
   * e. equality.

6. Lee acquired the ox he intended to slaughter for the !Kung Christmas feast
   * a. from Herero pastoralists living nearby.
   b. from a South African cattle rancher.
   c. from the !Kung headman.
   d. by catching it in the wild.
   e. none of the above.

8

Article 3

Shakespeare in the Bush
LAURA BOHANNAN

Summary This article illustrates the concept of *naive realism*, the idea that members of one group believe that everyone else sees the world they way they do, and shows how this belief leads to cross-cultural misunderstanding. Convinced that the basic theme of Shakespeare's *Hamlet* can be understood by people everywhere, Bohannan tries to tell the story to Tiv elders during fieldwork in West Africa. From the beginning, she finds that the Tiv translate the story into their own cultural categories. Since the Tiv have no spirits of the dead who can talk, they believe Hamlet's father's ghost is really an omen sent by a witch, or a zombie. Instead of committing an impropriety, Hamlet's mother did well to marry her dead husband's brother within a month of her spouse's death. The Tiv employ the levirate on such occasions, so that it is proper for a woman to marry her dead husband's brother. The Tiv think Polonius should be pleased that Hamlet wishes to have his daughter Ophelia. If they cannot marry, she can at least become his mistress, and sons of chiefs give large gifts to the fathers of their mistresses among the Tiv. At each turn in the story, the Tiv view events as they would in their own society, identifying facts according to their own cultural map and reinterpreting motives. The result is a very different *Hamlet* than Shakespeare wrote, and an excellent example of how culture defines a people's social world.

QUESTIONS

True or False?

F   1.   Bohannan finds that with minor alterations in terminology, Shakespeare's *Hamlet* can be understood in the same way by the English and the Tiv.

T   2.   The Tiv lack a concept for what Europeans call a ghost.

F   3.   The Tiv felt it was a good omen for Hamlet's father's ghost to return and talk with Hamlet.

T   4.   The Tiv approved of Hamlet's mother's marriage to her husband's brother within a month of the former's death.

T   5.   The Tiv felt that Laertes bewitched his sister, Ophelia, so that he could sell her body to raise money to repay gambling debts.

Multiple Choice

1. In her article, "Shakespeare in the Bush," Laura Bohannan shows that
    * a. the story of *Hamlet* does not retain its original meaning when told to a Tiv audience.
    b. the story of *Hamlet* retains Shakespeare's meaning for both the English and the Tiv.
    c. the Tiv misunderstand the meaning of Hamlet's gift of a Christmas ox.
    d. the Tiv understood why Hamlet's father's ghost would seek revenge.
    e. the Tiv were shocked by the quick marriage of Hamlet's mother to his uncle.

2. One of the concepts that the Tiv found it necessary to reinterpret when they were told the story of *Hamlet* was the English category for
    a. revenge.
    b. honor.
    c. omen.
    d. zombie.
    * e. ghost.

3. Four of the following describe ways the Tiv interpreted the story of *Hamlet*? Which one does **not**?
    a. The Tiv felt that the ghost of Hamlet's father was really an omen sent by a witch.
    b. The Tiv decided that Laertes killed his sister, Ophelia, through witchcraft.
    c. The Tiv were pleased by the quick marriage of Hamlet's mother to her dead husband's brother.
    * d. The Tiv approved of Hamlet's desire to kill his father's brother.
    e. The Tiv felt that Polonius' own error caused his death.

4. When the Tiv informed Laura Bohannan that she must be wrong about Hamlet's father's ghost because the dead cannot talk, they displayed what anthropologists call
    a. culture shock.
    * b. naive realism.
    c. ethnography.
    d. tacit culture.
    e. cross-cultural solidarity.

5. According to Bohannan, the Tiv approved of
    a. Hamlet's desire to kill his father's brother.
    b. Hamlet's desire to kill Polonius.
    c. Ophelia's attraction to Polonius.
    d. Hamlet's hasty marriage to Ophilia.
    * e. Hamlet's mother's hasty marriage to her dead husband's brother.

6. According to Bohannan (Shakespeare in the Bush), Tiv elders felt that Laertes
    * a. bewitched his sister, Ophelia, so he could sell her body to raise money to repay gambling debts.
      b. was killed by Hamlet when he refused to identify himself, something any good hunter would do if there was a chance of being mistaken for game.
      c. sent a zombie to hurt Hamlet.
      d. married Ophelia too quickly after the death of her husband.
      e. was turned into a zombie by his sister, Ophelia, who was jealous of the attention he paid to Hamlet.

Article 4

Fieldwork on Prostitution in the Era of AIDS   CLAIRE E. STERK

Summary This article discusses ethnographic fieldwork as a process—entering the field, making contact, developing rapport, interviewing, and experiencing stress. It also illustrates the adaptation of anthropology and anthropologists to fieldwork in complex U.S. microcultures (in this case the culture of prostitutes), illustrating how participant observation, originally developed by anthropologists to discover the content of nonwestern cultures, can be adapted for use at home.

The subjects of Sterk's study were "low end" prostitutes, those who worked the streets and crack houses. Research was conducted over several years and involved 180 informants. To begin the study, Sterk talked to police, health care people, and community representatives in an effort to locate and gain introductions to prostitutes and to develop an ethnographic map of where prostitution occurred. Hanging out on the street, she met and gained rapport with some prostitutes, and through them and their pimps, met many more. Lessons from this contact period included advice to go slowly, and to have some knowledge of the scene but to avoid appearing to be an expert. Sterk also learned that gatekeepers (people who give you access to other informants) become less important as time goes by, that some give you access to only part of a cultural scene, that some key informants are not well connected after all, and that key informants can be a problem when association with them cuts off access to others. Watch out especially for self-nominated key informants she cautions.

Developing rapport was best done by hanging out and doing things for people, such as giving them rides and buying groceries for them. Eventually, many women were flattered by Sterk's interest in them. Rapport was enhanced by encouraging women to have some control over the research process. This meant letting informants tell their own stories and refraining from dominating interviews. Interviews were conducted in private and required consent forms, which surprisingly did not bother informants. Authority figures who controlled prostitutes, in this case usually pimps, sometimes presented an impediment to research.

Fieldwork involved stress, which was partially relieved by leaving the field every day. But leaving the field also caused feelings of guilt as did the informant deaths from AIDS.

The article ends with six observations about prostitutes and their culture. Prostitutes often blame past experiences for their current status and alienation from "normal" people outside the life. There are different kinds of prostitutes—treetwalkers, women hooked on drugs after they started the profession, women who entered the life already addicted to drugs, and women who turned tricks as payment for drugs. Most prostitutes worked for a pimp. AIDS affects their lives but condom use was a problem for customers. Men are often violent toward prostitutes. Finally, women do leave the life but their past often follows them like a bad hangover.

QUESTIONS

True or False?

F 1. According to Sterk in her article, "Prostitution in the Era of AIDS," virtually all the prostitutes she interviewed or observed were hooked on drugs.

T 2. According to Sterk, 30 prostitutes she interviewed were college graduates and 75 percent of her informants had graduated from high school.

F 3. Sterk (Prostitution in the Era of AIDS) found that it is essential to become an expert on the lives of informants before interviewing them and to use such informant to design interview questions.

T 4. Finding informant sites, making contact, dealing with self-appointed key informants, gaining rapport, and leaving the field were all important challenges to doing ethnographic fieldwork among prostitutes.

F 5. Sterk (Prostitution in the Era of AIDS) found it was essential to interview prostitutes in the presence of their pimps and other prostitutes in order to gain trust.

T 6. Sterk found that AIDS affects the lives of prostitutes but that customers often refuse to use condoms.

F 7. According to Sterk, the greatest impediment to developing rapport in field is the requirement, imposed by her university, that informants sign consent forms.

Multiple Choice

1. Sterk ("Fieldwork on Prostitution in the Era of AIDS) argues that
   * a. it is essential to act like an authority when you interview informants.
   b. initial contacts in the field are often referred to as gatekeepers and key respondents by anthropologists.
   c. it is important to watch out for self-nominated key informants.
   d. the best way to gain rapport is to show interest in people and do things for them.
   e. in depth interviews should be done in private.

2. According to Sterk (Fieldwork on Prostitution in the Era of AIDS), about _____ percent of the prostitutes she interviewed were not drug addicts.
   a. 10
   * b. 25
   c. 2
   d. 40
   e. 15

3. Sterk (Fieldwork on Prostitution in the Era of AIDS) makes several observations about gatekeepers. Which one of the following is **not** one of her observations? Gatekeepers are
   a. important to getting started in fieldwork.
 * b. may become less important to a study as time goes on.
   c. make the best key informants.
   d. may give you access to only part of a cultural scene.
   e. may not be well connected after all.

4. Four of the following statements made by Sterk (Fieldwork on Prostitution in the Era of AIDS), are true. Which one is **not**?
   a. It is wise to watch out for self-appointed "gatekeepers."
   b. The best way to gain rapport is to show interest in informants and do things for them.
   c. Have some knowledge about a culture before you start fieldwork in it.
 * d. Talking with informants in groups often inhibits ethnographic discovery.
   e. It is best to give informants some control over the interview.

5. Sterk listed several conclusions about prostitutes and prostitution based on her field study. Which one of the following is **not** a conclusion she reached.
   a. men are often violent toward prostitutes.
   b. women do leave "the life," but their past often follows them like a bad hangover.
   c. most prostitutes work for a pimp.
   d. first experiences as prostitutes often involve alienation from people outside the life.
 * e. although police and health professionals insist that prostitutes are drug addicts, most are not.

6. When Sterk (Fieldwork on Prostitution in the Era of AIDS) first tried to make contact with prostitutes in the street, they
   a. disappeared, walking to other locations.
   b. became angry and tried to drive her away with threats.
 * c. largely ignored her.
   d. called their pimps on cell phones and their pimps threatened her.
   e. welcomed her warmly because she was interested in their lives.

7. Sterk (Fieldwork on Prostitution in the Era of Aids) found that in-depth interviews
   a. worked best if she had asked a list of carefully prepared questions.
 * b. worked best if held in private.
   c. yielded little in-depth information.
   d. were the most stressful part of fieldwork.
   e. yielded too many contradictions to be useful.

Article 5

Lessons from the Field   GEORGE GMELCH

Summary This article, which is a revision and update of the one published in the ninth edition of *Conformity and Conflict*, is based on the author's 18 years of experience with an undergraduate field research program sponsored by Union College. It looks at the adjustment students have had to make living with families on the Caribbean island of Barbados, and the effect the field experience has had on them personally. The article provides an inside view of the nature of culture and cultural differences from the student perspective. In this way, it illustrates the reflexive nature of ethnography research.

Gmelch argues that fieldwork affects students in seven important ways. First, his students, most of whom are from U.S. suburbs, discover what it is like to live in a rural setting. They learn about life in rural settings, including the importance of farming and the natural environment, a strong sense of community, the slow pace of life, lack of anonymity, occupational pluralism (people work at several jobs to make a living), and intimate social relations. Second, they discover through residence in poor communities that they can live happily without material wealth, and express discomfort at the abundance of their own possessions when they return home to the United States. Third, students, especially females, must adjust to Bajan (Barbadian) sexual behaviors. Bajan men make open comments about women, who tolerate or are flattered by the attention. Dancing is erotic and women, much more than in the United States, are treated as subordinates and sexual objects. Fourth, students discover what it is like to be members of a racial minority (most students are white, most Barbadians are black). Although they tend to forget about their race after a few weeks in the field, many white students claim that the field experience gives them a new affinity for black people once they return home. Fifth, students expand their understanding of the concept of social class. Beginning fieldwork with the idea that there are no classes on Barbados, students soon discover class differences (Rastas are low, for example) and that they have to be careful to associate with the "right" people. Sixth, students begin to see people and life in the United States in a different light. They are embarrassed by the behavior of U.S. tourists, who seem to care so little about Barbadian culture and who dress immodestly, solicit sex, and speak too loudly. They see the increase in prostitution, crime, and drug abuse related to tourism. Seventh, Gmelch observes that field experience makes his students more serious about their education, both because they see the value of their own fieldwork and because Barbadians value education so highly. In closing, he extols the virtues of the multicultural experience and the value of fieldwork to teach student researchers about themselves.

QUESTIONS

True or False?

T   1.   In his article, "Lessons from the Field," George Gmelch claims that fieldwork in Barbados teaches undergraduate students what it is like to be a racial minority.

F   2.   Gmelch argues that student field workers from the United States expect to find social classes on Barbados, and are surprised by Barbadian egalitarianism.

T   3.   Gmelch claims that U.S. student fieldworkers discover that they can live without many material possessions when they are in Barbados.

F   4.   Gmelch notes that U.S. students are depressed by the high levels of poverty on Barbados and by the fact that most men and women are unemployed.

T   5.   Gmelch notes that student field workers become more critical of their own country, particularly the U.S. tourists who dress immodestly by Barbadian standards, are loud, and are ignorant of local customs.

F   6.   Gmelch notes that unlike America, female students find that they can go anywhere on Barbados and be treated with respect by both men and women.

Multiple Choice

1.   According to Gmelch (Lessons From the Field), female U.S. student fieldworkers find that men living on Barbados usually
     a.   treat them with respect.
 * b.   regard them as subordinates.
     c.   are hostile toward them because they are white.
     d.   two of the above.
     e.   none of the above.

2.   According to Gmelch, U.S. undergraduate fieldworkers come to learn four of the following things when they do research on Barbados. Which one is **not** something they learn?
 * a.   what life is like to live in an egalitarian society.
     b.   that it is possible to live and be happy without an abundance of material goods.
     c.   what it is like to be a racial minority.
     d.   that it can be pleasant to live where the pace of life is slow.
     e.   that education is something to be respected and taken seriously.

3. According to Gmelch, U.S. students learn that rural life on Barbados is marked by four of the following. Which one is it **not** marked by?
   a.   a closeness with nature
 * b.   social equality
   c.   a slow pace of life
   d.   multiple stranded social relationships
   e.   lack of anonymity

4. After a few weeks working on Barbados, U.S. students become critical of North American tourists. Four of the following are criticisms of U.S. tourists by Barbadians. Which one is **not**?
   a.   women come to Barbados for sexual encounters
   b.   women dress immodestly
   c.   tourists talk too loudly
 * d.   tourists are too friendly and push themselves on Barbadians
   e.   tourists know little about and seem hardly interested in Barbadian culture

5. One of the drawbacks of rural life that U.S. undergraduate fieldworkers find it most difficult to adjust to is
   a.   being white in a black country.
   b.   maintaining sexual modesty.
   c.   the slow pace of life.
   d.   local poverty.
 * e.   the lack of anonymity and privacy.

6. According to Gmelch (Lessons from the Field), four of the following are true about Barbadian society. Which one is **not**?
   a.   Barbadian women are more likely to be unemployed
   b.   Barbadian women may be flattered when men yell out comments about them in public
   c.   Barbadian women shrug off the hissing that some young men direct their way in public
   d.   Barbadian women often imitate intercourse (grind) when they dance in public with men
 * e.   Barbadian women often hold public office because they are more likely to vote

PART 2

LANGUAGE AND COMMUNICATION

Part 2 introduces the following important concepts associated with language and speech, and with other aspects and forms of communication.

KEY DEFINITIONS

A **symbol** is anything people can perceive with their senses that stands for something else.

Language is a system of cultural knowledge used to generate and interpret speech.

Speech refers to the behavior that produces vocal sounds.

Phonology consists of the categories and rules for forming vocal symbols.

Phonemes are the minimal categories of speech sounds that serve to keep utterances apart.

Grammar refers to the categories and rules for combining vocal symbols.

Morphemes are the minimal units of meaning in any language.

Semantics refers to the categories and rules for relating vocal symbols to their referents.

Sociolinguistic rules combine meaningful utterances with social situations into appropriate messages.

Nonlinguistic symbols are symbols outside of language that carry meaning for human beings.

QUESTIONS

True or False?

F   1.   Language refers to the behavior that produces vocal sounds.

T   2.   Language is a system of cultural knowledge used to generate and interpret speech.

F 3. Things other than vocal sounds that can stand for other things are part of language.

T 4. The minimal categories of speech sounds that serve to keep utterances apart are called phonemes.

F 5. Grammar refers to the categories and rules for linking vocal symbols with their referents.

T 6. People can communicate using nonlinguistic symbols.

Multiple Choice

1. The behavior that produces vocal sounds is called
    a. semantics.
    b. language.
    * c. speech.
    d. phonology.
    e. morphology.

2. The system of cultural knowledge used to generate and interpret speech is called
    a. communication.
    * b. language.
    c. semantics.
    d. phonology.
    e. grammar.

3. Like all symbols, vocal symbols must
    a. have a referent.
    b. occur in minimal pairs.
    c. be perceivable by our senses.
    * d. two of the above.
    e. a, b, and c above.

4. Minimal categories of speech that serve to keep utterances apart are called
    a. morphemes.
    b. minimal pairs.
    c. words.
    * d. phonemes.
    e. phones.

5. Hindi speakers hear which of the following two English phonemes as a single phoneme?
    a. /t/ and /d/
    b. /k/ and /g/
    c. /b/ and /d/
    d. /l/ and /r/
  * e. /v/ and /w/

6. The categories and rules for combining vocal symbols are called
    a. phonemes.
  * b. grammar.
    c. phonology.
    d. sociolinguistic rules.
    e. speech.

Article 6

Homo grammaticus

MARTIN A. NOWAK

Summary Mathematical linguist, Martin Nowak, makes several useful generalizations about human spoken language in this article. He notes that our language permits us to speak about anything, whether sensed or imagined. He argues that people use an innate (inherited) grammatical ability to combine a limited number of sounds and sound combinations into an infinite number of utterances. He indicates that mathematical models can demonstrate the adaptive utility of a grammatical system, which explains its evolutionary advantage for our species.

He begins by observing that his four- and six-year-old sons' language is limited by neither experience nor worldly context. They, and indeed everyone, can talk about anything. Humans learn to speak rapidly by talking and hearing examples of sentences. By four they will have mastered a basic set of sound categories (phonemes) and are able to avoid 95 percent of the grammatical errors they could make. As they grow they learn a new word every 90 minutes; by age seventeen they control a lexicon of about 50,000 words. The ability, which linguist Noam Chomsky calls *universal grammar*, to learn the grammar that organizes language is built-in.

Grammar refers to the patterns inherent in speech sounds, word forms, and sentence structures (syntax). The aim of the article is to show through the use of mathematical equations, how grammar evolved. Language is a key to human evolution. All people have the same language ability, which evolved at least by 150,000 to 200,000 years ago. Earlier primate languages and indeed those of many animals communicate through sounds that refer to specific things—people, objects, actions, places, times, and events. Using a mathematical equation, it is possible to show that as the number of sounds for different things multiplies, communicative mistakes increase until a limit is reached beyond which communication becomes an adaptive liability. Non human communication systems are essentially capped at a simple level by this problem.

Human language overcame this liability by evolving grammar. Most human languages keep the number of speech sounds to a low number, usually 40 or less. But we increase the ability of this small number of sounds to refer to things by combining them into words. This "two level" system means that a language can have many thousands (English has about 100,000) of words. These, in turn, can be grammatically combined in a variety of ways to produce longer sentences. Following the grammatical rules of our language, we can all say things that have never been said before, and refer to new things and to past or future events and far-off places. It is easy to show with a second mathematical equation that our grammatically-based language confers adaptive advantage, but only if we need to talk about a large variety of things. Humans reached this level, called the *syntax threshold*, and evolved grammar; other animals have not reached this threshold. Finally, grammatical language has enabled humans to produce a new kind of evolution that is cultural.

QUESTIONS

True or False?

T 1. According to Nowak (*Homo grammaticus*), by the time they are seventeen years old, most people will have a lexicon of about 50,000 words.

F 2. Nowak (*Homo grammaticus*) argues that there is a mathematical limitation on the number things people can say.

F 3. According to Nowak, humans are not born with the potential to learn and use grammar.

T 4. According to Nowak(*Homo grammaticus*), animal communications systems have a one-to-one relationship between the events and things that can be sensed and the sounds that refer to them.

T 5. Nowak claims that other animals have not evolved a grammatical system of communication because they have not reached the syntactic threshold.

F 6. According to Nowak, humans learn a syntactical structure that enables them to memorize a large number of sentences that refer to specific events or other things they can sense.

Multiple Choice

1. According to Nowak (*Homo grammaticus*), four of the following are attributes of human language learning. Which one is **not**?
    a. Four-year-olds know how to avoid 95 percent of the grammatical mistakes they could make.
    b. Children have learned about 13,000 words by the time they are six years old.
    * c. Children up to the age of four can usually speak about things they can sense (see, hear, touch, smell).
    d. Humans are born with an innate (inherited) grammatical sense.
    e. By the time they reach the age of seventeen, people will have learned about 50,000 words.

2. Nowak (*Homo grammaticus*), following linguist Noam Chomsky, argues that
    a. languages vary according to their ability to reflect reality.
    * b. children are born with *universal grammar*, a built-in sense of what grammar is.
    c. most languages use between 50 and 70 phonemic sound categories.
    d. languages spoken by hunter/gathers and horticulturalists are less likely to permit the expression of abstract thought.
    e. it is likely that some animal languages, ones used by dolphins, for example, also share grammatical structure similar to human language.

3. According to Nowak (*Homo grammaticus*), animals, such as wolves, dolphins, and chimpanzees
    * a. are linguistically limited by a one-to-one relationship between sounds and their referents.
    b. can be taught to speak in ways that are as complex as our own language.
    c. are unable to communicate.
    d. communicate using a limited number of sound groupings
    e. often misunderstand each other because of the complexity of their sound and gesture system.

4. According to Nowak (*Homo grammaticus*), the term, "universal grammar," (coined by Noam Chomsky), means the
    a. grammatical system developed by linguists to create a universal language.
    b. system of common words found in all human languages.
    c. fundamental need of humans everywhere to communicate with each other.
    d. system of gestures, emotions, and facial expressions shared by all human beings.
    * e. built-in sense of what grammar is that is shared by people everywhere.

5. In his article, *Homo grammaticus*, Nowak defines the "syntactical threshold" as
    a. the grammatical complexity limit human language can attain.
    b. the level of complexity a grammatical system must attain in order to become an effective means of communication
    c. the lowest number of sound categories (phonemes) it takes to form words.
    * d. the number of things a species needs to communicate that requires adoption of a grammatical system.
    e. the lowest number of strategies it takes for young people to learn grammar.

Article 7

Body Art as Visual Language

ENID SCHILDKROUT

Summary Enid Schildkrout wrote this piece (actually two related articles) for *AnthroNotes* to coincide with the opening of an exhibit on body art developed by the American Museum of Natural History. The article describes body art as a universal, visual system of communication, and it lists and describes its various forms and their communicative functions.

Body art is old. 30,000-year-old European cave paintings suggest the presence of body painting. Ornaments from many ancient sites were worn through body piercings. Mummies, such as the "ice man," were tattooed. Body art is visual and a human universal; it is found in every society, but it is also culturally produced and its meanings may be exclusive to particular cultures. Body art makes a statement about the person who wears it and it may symbolize a variety of things from depictions of heroic epochs and personal rank to group identity and personal rebellion. As forms of body art move from one society to another, however, they may lose their original meanings and gain new ones. Body art may be permanent (scarification, tattoos, piercing) or temporary (hair styles, lipstick, body painting).

There are many kinds of body art. Body painting, which often codes symbolic meaning in color and design; makeup, which may convey beauty and sexual difference or camouflage imperfections; hair styling, shaving or cutting, which can indicate mourning, identity change, and even rebellion; scarification (cicatrisation), which alters the skin by cutting or branding and often indicates a permanent change in status; tattooing, the insertion of ink or pigment under the top layer of skin, which may be decorative but signal such things as group membership and rank and which is a persistent and universal form of body art; piercing, the insertion of objects through the skin, which is also very common and often part of a ritual status change, are all forms of body art.

Body art has many functions. It may link individuals with ancestors, deities, and spirits, mediate relationship with the supernatural, shield individuals from evil or attract good luck, serve as maps of terrain, or mark a transition in social status. The meanings of body art are changing with travel. Body art can be used to form new identities and signal social conformity or rebellion.

QUESTIONS

True or False?

F   1.   In her article on body art, Schildkraut argues that even the numbers tattooed on concentration camp inmates can be classified as body art.

T   2.   According to Schildkraut (Body Art), athe body is the oldest canvas for art.

F 3. In her selection, "Body Art," Schildkraut notes that the original meanings of body art tend to persist when the art forms move from one society to another.

T 4. According to Schildkraut (Body Art), Chinese tattoos often depicted epics known by common people while Polynesians used tattoos to indicate rank.

F 5. Schildkraut (Body Art) claims that body shaping has the greatest potential to transform a person into someone else.

T 6. Schildkraut (Body Art) says that neck rings, breast implants, rib aremoval and tiny waists, bound feet, and elongated heads are all kinds of body shaping.

F 7. Schildkraut (Body Art) notes that tattooing is one of the rarest forms of body art.

Multiple Choice

1. In her article, "Body Art," Schildkraut argues that
    * a. body shaping (neck rings, breast implants, bound tiny feet) is a form of body art.
    b. the rarest form of body art is body painting.
    c. altering the body in a temporary fashion (cosmetics, body painting, hair dying) does not produce true body art.
    d. several societies lack body art.
    e. even numbers tattooed on the arms of concentration inmates are a form of body art.

2. According to Schildkraut (Body Art), four of the following statements about body art are true. Which one is **not**?
    a. Body painting has the greatest potential to transform a person into someone else.
    b. Cicatrisation alters the skin by cutting or branding.
    c. breast implants are a form of body art.
    d. body art is a visual language.
    * e. numbers tattooed on concentration camp inmates are a form of body art.

3. According and Schildkraut (Body Art), cutting of the skin is called
    a. piercing.
    * b. cicatrisation.
    c. body shaping.
    d. body painting.
    e. makeup.

4. Schildkraut (Body Art) says that _____ is **not** a function of body art found in at least a few societies.
   a. linking people with their ancestors.
   b. serving as maps of terrain.
   * c. identifying sex offender jail inmates.
   d. marking a transition in social status
   e. signaling rebellion.

5. Schildkraut (Body Art) notes that some New Yorkers have tattoos that originate in Borneo and serve as a sign of rebellion. In Borneo the tattoos
   a. serve to distinguish men from women.
   b. indicate clan membership.
   c. signal rank.
   * d. light the path of a person's soul after death.
   e. illustrate the exploits of a gangster hero.

6. Four of the following statements about body are made by anthropologist Enid Schildkraut (Body Art) are true. Which one is not? Body is
   a. often misunderstood across cultures.
   b. a way to indicate group membership.
   c. a way to indicate the transformation of an individual from one social identity to another.
   * d. based on a universal cultural ideals of beauty.
   e. is either temporary or permanent.

Article 8

Worlds Shaped by Words

DAVID S. THOMSON

Summary In this article, David Thomson discusses the Sapir-Whorf hypothesis first introduced by Benjamin Lee Whorf. As a counter to the notion that languages simple code reality, Whorf argued that both grammar and words can determine reality. Whorf, an insurance inspector who was also an accomplished linguist, illustrated this point with many examples, including the famous case of "empty" gasoline drums that nevertheless will blow up if you throw a cigarette into them (there is no English word for empty but not empty), and his analysis of Hopi grammatical tenses which, he claimed, cause Hopi Indians to see the world in two modes, what has become and becoming.

Tests of Whorf's hypothesis using color categories seem to show that people can more easily remember and recognize phenomena for which they have words. People with many words for things seem to be able to perceive the coded differences more quickly.

Yet critics of Whorf argue that while languages may permit easier discourse about some things, all people can perceive the same things, thus language does not determine perception. In addition, they argue that Whorf used dead metaphors, such as "goodbye," which does not now mean the religious world view its root, "God be with you," might imply.

Thomson concludes his article with a discussion of how we use words to manipulate perception. For example, people can use such terms as "boy" to degrade African American men, and euphemisms, such as "bathroom" and "protective reaction strike," to hide the stark realities of bodily functions and bombing villages. In this sense, Whorf's ideas seem to apply at least in a modified way.

QUESTIONS

True or False?

T   1.   According to David Thomson, linguist Benjamin Lee Whorf argued that instead of simply - labeling experience, language could actually determine how people perceive reality.

F   2.   According to Thomson, the Sapir-Whorf hypothesis argues that language labels experience; it does not determine human perception.

T   3.   In his discussion of Whorf's hypothesis, Thomson argues that it is impossible to prove that language determines perception.

F   4.   In his discussion of Whorf's hypothesis, Thomson reports that words for colors determine which colors members of societies are able to perceive.

F   5.   In his discussion of Whorf's hypothesis, Thomson notes that euphemisms, such as "protective reaction strike," cannot change the meaning of their referents, in this case the bombing of villages.

Multiple Choice

1.   Thomson discusses a theory by Benjamin Lee Whorf that suggests languages
   a.   label reality.
   b.   serve to demarcate social groups.
 * c.   determine perception.
   d.   reflect personality.
   e.   are randomly patterned.

2.   Thomson notes that Whorf worked with _____ grammar and found that the language did not have a past, present, and future tense.
   a.   Hanunoo
   b.   German
   c.   English
   d.   Yiddish
 * e.   Hopi.

3.   Thomson notes which one of the following is an important criticism of Whorf's work?
 * a.   Its uncritical interpretation of dead metaphors.
   b.   The fact that large numbers of words, such as Hanunoo categories for types of rice, do not affect perception as Whorf would have argued.
   c.   The fact that it is difficult to translate one language neatly into another.
   d.   The fact that the Hanunoo would have difficulty discriminating among U.S. cars.
   e.   The use of Hopi examples.

4.   Which one of the following words mentioned by Thomson serves as an example of a dead metaphor?
   a.   Cary Grant (originally Archibald Leach)
 * b.   goodbye
   c.   boy (as used by whites for African American men)
   d.   billiard parlor (for "pool hall")
   e.   the people (to refer to one's nationality)

5.   According to Thomson, Whorf found that Hopi grammar reflected an adjustment to
   a.   war.
   b.   pastoralism.
   c.   urban living.
 * d.   agriculture.
   e.   foraging.

Article 9

The Military Name Game
SARAH BOXER

Summary The previous article by Thomson reviews Whorf's theory that language can shape human perception. Although critics have challenged this idea, it is clear that people regularly try to use language to influence the meaning of things and events, and they are more likely to succeed if people know little about what is being described. In this piece, Sarah Boxer, using information contained in an article entitled "The Art of Naming Operations" by Lt. Col. Gregory C. Sieminski, shows how military operations' names have shifted in purpose from an inside code to a public symbol meant to motivate people. The Germans initiated the naming of operations as an inside secret code. The British did the same, but with rules laid down by Winston Churchill who felt operations names should neither be boastful nor despondent or frivolous. After World War II the Pentagon started to create names for public consumption and with them, controversies about what names should convey. During the Korean conflict, for example, General Macarthur used aggressive names, such as "thunderbolt" and "ripper" for operations. The Vietnam War saw Lyndon Johnson veto aggressive names; for him, "masher" sounded too aggressive and he replaced it with "white wing." Following Vietnam, the Pentagon bureaucracy codified the process. Each command was given some two-letter sequences that would start two-word operations names. Further, the Pentagon developed a computer program entitled "Code Word, Nickname, and Exercise Term System" (called "NICKA" for short). Modern operations naming involves a verb-noun sequence—"promote liberty," "Restore Hope"—which may seem boring but can be important because they can become the name for a whole war. Since almost any choice of words seems to offend someone, Boxer concludes that the new game is to find words without meaning.

QUESTIONS

True or False?

F   1.   According to Boxer (The Military Name Game), names for military operations have little effect on the way the public perceives such actions.

T   2.   According to Boxer (The Military Name Game), the military uses a two-word verb-noun sequence to describe military operations.

F   3.   Boxer (The Military Name Game) asserts that the original purpose of naming military operations was to generate public approval for them.

T   4.   According to Boxer (The Military Name Game), despite every effort to make them benign, most recent attempts at naming military operations manage to offend someone.

F   5.   Boxer (The Military Name Game) shows how a modern computer program entitled "Code Word, Nickname, and Exercise Term System," or NICKA for short, has solved most of the problems encountered by the Pentagon as it generates code names for military operations.

T   6.   According to Boxer (The Military Name Game), code names for military operations originated with the Germans in World War II and were intended to be secret.

Multiple Choice

1.   In her article, "The Military Name Game," Boxer argues that today, naming military operations involves using
  * a.   a two-word verb-noun phrase that is positive but that is almost meaningless
    b.   mythology and religion because of their positive moral overtones.
    c.   words that are intended to remain secret.
    d.   consultants from the private sector with backgrounds in advertising.
    e.   aggressive terms such as "Masher," "Thunderbolt," and "Ripper."

2.   According to Boxer (The Military Name Game), the first name given to U.S. operations in Afghanistan was
    a.   Desert Storm
    b.   Mountain Shield
    c.   Just Cause
    d.   Enduring Freedom
  * e.   Infinite Justice

3.   According and Boxer (The Military Name Game), the U.S. Joint Chiefs of Staff created a _____ nicknamed _____ to generate names for military operations.
    a.   military command committee: "COMAT"
  * b.   computer program: "NICKA"
    c.   three-service bureau; "BOCAB"
    d.   military swat team: "SWATNOM"
    e.   none of the above

4.   Boxer (The Military Name Game), notes that the name for U.S. operations in Afghanistan, "Infinite Justice," was dropped because
    a.   the term, "infinite," implied that the operation would go on forever.
    b.   the term, "justice," implied a legal rationale for pursuing the conflict and there was none.
    c.   the phrase was too general and meaningless.
  * d.   the Council on American-Islamic Relations felt it implied a godly role for the U.S.
    e.   the phrase angered the U.S.'s Arab allies.

5. According to Boxer (The Military Name Game), military operations names such as Roundup, Killer, Ripper, Courageous, Audacious and Dauntless were used by _____ during _____.

* a. General Macarthur: the Korean War
  b. Winston Churchill: World War II
  c. General Abrams: the Vietnam War
  d. President Reagan: the invasion of Granada
  e. Joint Chiefs of Staff: the war with Iraq

Article 10

Conversation Style: Talking on the Job   DEBORAH TANNEN

Summary In this selection excerpted from her book, *Talking from 9 to 5*, Deborah Tannen describes misunderstandings in the work place based on the different *speaking styles* of men and women. Tannen notes that most people blame miscommunication on the intentions, different abilities, and character of others, or on their own failure or the failure of the relationship. Miscommunication in the work place, however, often occurs between men and women because gender is a basic indicator of identity and because men and women learn different styles of speaking.

Tannen introduces an example of gender-based misunderstanding in which a female manager uses first praise, then suggestions to criticize a male employee's report. Her comments are misunderstood by the employee as praise and miscommunication occurs. The manager thinks she is diplomatic; the employee thinks she is dishonest. The differences, argues Tanner, have to do with different styles of speaking. Men avoid being put in a one down position by using oppositions such as banter, joking, teasing, and playful put-downs. Women seek the appearance of equality and try to avoid flexing their muscles to get jobs done. The misunderstandings occur when actors take each other's speaking styles literally.

The remainder of the selection deals with a particular male speaking style, the reluctance to ask directions. Women ask directions because it seems to be the fastest way to get things done. Men hesitate to ask questions, claiming that they develop their navigation skills by going at things independently. Tanner argues that men avoid asking because it puts them in a one down position. Each style can have its pitfalls. Male pilots or doctors who fail to ask questions may endanger their own or other people's lives. Female doctors and managers who ask too many questions may risk signaling that they are tentative or unsure of themselves.

Tannen concludes by saying that neither style is inherently wrong, just different, and that speakers should be aware of gender-based speaking styles and flexible in their own use of them.

QUESTIONS

True or False?

F   1.   Tannen, in her selection, "Conversation Style: Talking on the Job," claims that women's speaking styles, based on a need to create the appearance of equality, are a better form of communication in the work place than men's more direct speaking styles.

T   2.   According to Tannen (Conversation Style: Talking on the Job), speaking styles are ritualized forms of verbal interaction that often differ between men and women.

F 3. In her selection, "Conversation Style: Talking on the Job," Tannen argues that most people blame misunderstandings on the ambivalence of words used by men and women when they talk at work.

T 4. According to Tannen (Conversation Style: Talking on the Job), most people think that miscommunication is caused by the intention, different capabilities, and character of others, or by their own failure or a poor relationship.

F 5. Tannen (Conversation Style: Talking on the Job) claims that men's failure to ask for directions is a serious flaw in communications between the sexes in the workplace and should be changed.

T 6. Tannen (Conversation Style: Talking on the Job) argues that in the workplace, men often refrain from asking for directions because it puts them in a one-down position.

Multiple Choice

1. In her article, "Conversation Style: Talking on the Job," Tannen argues that in the workplace
    * a. men often refrain from asking for directions while women often seek to create the appearance of equality in a conversation.
    b. men believe that women are too forward and direct when they talk.
    c. gender does not affect talking styles.
    d. women seek a one up position in conversation whereas men diffuse speech domination by joking about it.
    e. men are more likely than women to ask for directions.

2. According to Tannen, women's conversation often works at the appearance of equality. Men's conversation, on the other hand, is often directed at
    a. an attempt to put others in a one-down position by bragging or inferring superior knowledge.
    b. avoiding the one-down position by acting as if they don't know what the other person means.
    c. avoiding the one-down position by ignoring other people.
    d. an attempt to put others in a one-down position by faking interest in the conversation.
    * e. avoiding the one-down position by using oppositions such as banter, joking, teasing, and playful putdowns.

3. According and Tannen, men often avoid asking directions because
    a. their over-direct style does not yield accurate answers.
    * b. asking puts them in a one-down position.
    c. they fail to listen to the answers they get.
    d. two of the above.
    e. none of the above.

4. Tannen (Conversation Style: Talking on the Job), tells the story of how Amy, a manager, tried to tell her employee, Donald, how to change an unsatisfactory report. Her approach led to misunderstanding because
    a. she was too direct.
    b. Donald would not ask for help.
 * c. she praised the good parts of the report before suggesting changes.
    d. she put Donald in a one-down position by demonstrating her superior knowledge.
    e. Donald took her comments as a personal criticism.

5. Tannen (Conversation Style: Talking on the Job), notes that of all the examples of conversational-style differences between men and women that lead to troublesome outcomes, _____ has attracted the most attention of her readers.
    a. men's tendency to interrupt women in normal conversation
    b. women's tendency to criticize men when they talk with each other
    c. women's tendency to be indirect when they talk with men
 * d. men's tendency to avoid asking directions of other people
    e. men's tendency to act as if they know the answer to a question when they actually don't

6. Tannen argues that one negative consequence for women of asking questions is that they may seem
 * a. weak and unconfident.
    b. pushy and overbearing.
    c. cold and uncaring.
    d. two of the above.
    e. a, b, and c above.

7. According to Tannen, men often argue that an advantage of not asking questions is that
    a. they avoid receiving incorrect information.
    b. they learn to discover answers for themselves.
    c. they can feel superior to other people by not showing their ignorance.
 * d. two of the above.
    e. a, b, and c above.

8. Tannen notes that men often fail to ask for directions and that women usually do ask for directions. Since it is easy to show that not asking for directions can have dire consequences, she suggests that men
    a. should change, and ask directions.
    b. should ask directions, but in an indirect manner.
 * c. should be flexible, asking directions when it seems appropriate to do so.
    d. two of the above.
    e. none of the above.

PART 3

ECOLOGY AND SUBSISTENCE

The introduction to Part 3 discusses the concept of cultural ecology and a classification of societies based on their adaptive food-getting strategies.

KEY DEFINITIONS

Ecology is the relationship of an organism to other elements within its environmental sphere.

Cultural ecology refers to the way people use their culture to adapt to particular environments.

The **physical environment** is the world people experience with their senses.

The **cultural environment** is a people's cultural classification of their physical environment, which usually reflects their adaptive needs and other cultural values.

Subsistence strategies are strategies used by human groups to exploit their environment for material necessities.

Hunting and gathering (foraging) is an adaptive food-getting strategy based on the collecting of wild plants and the hunting of wild animals.

Horticulture is an adaptive strategy in which food is gardened with hoe or digging stick.

Slash-and-burn agriculture, sometimes also referred to as shifting agriculture, is a common kind of horticulture in which large trees are cut and the fields burned over before planting.

Pastoralism is an adaptive strategy based on the herding of domesticated animals such as cattle, sheep, or goats.

Agriculture is an adaptive strategy based on the intensive farming of permanent fields. Agriculture is often associated with the use of the plow, irrigation, and sometimes terracing.

Industrialism is subsistence strategies marked by intensive, mechanized food production and elaborate distribution networks.

QUESTIONS

True or False?

F   1.   The physical environment is one area of human experience that people everywhere categorize in the same way.

F   2.   Food-getting strategies have little impact on the structure of society.

T   3.   Four anthropological classifications of societies based on food-getting techniques are hunting and gathering, horticulture, pastoralism, and agriculture.

F   4.   The origin of bipedality (two-footedness) in humans is something that an anthropologist interested in cultural ecology would study.

T   5.   Slash-and-burn agriculture is a kind of horticulture.

F   6.   Cultural ecology is the most important form of subsistence strategy.

Multiple Choice

1.   The study of how people use their culture to adapt to particular environments is called
   a.   ecology.
 * b.   cultural ecology.
   c.   environmentalism.
   d.   environmental determinism.
   e.   physical ecology.

2.   The world that people can experience with their senses is called
   a.   ecology.
   b.   cultural ecology.
 * c.   physical environment.
   d.   cultural environment.
   e.   none of the above.

3.   The fact that a tourist sees scenic mountains and valleys when viewing a high pass in the Rocky Mountains, whereas a geologist sees cirque basins, U-shaped valleys, and paternoster streams, illustrates the concept of
   a.   ecosystem.
   b.   cultural ecology.
   c.   physical environment.
 * d.   cultural environment.
   e.   scientific impartiality.

4. Slash-and-burn agriculture would best be classified as a kind of which one of the following adaptive strategies?
   a. hunting and gathering
   * b. horticulture
   c. agriculture
   d. pastoralism
   e. industrialism

5. If a society uses irrigation, its food-getting (subsistence) system would best be classified as
   * a. agriculture.
   b. horticulture.
   c. pastoral.
   d. hunting and gathering.
   e. hydraulic.

6. Four of the following are listed as subsistence strategies in Part 3 of *Conformity and Conflict*. Which one of the following is **not**?
   a. pastoral
   b. hunting and gathering
   c. agricultural
   * d. manufacturing
   e. horticultural

7. Which one of the following subsistence strategies would most typically be found to support permanent settlements containing between 50 and 250 people?
   a. hunting and gathering
   * b. horticulture
   c. agriculture
   d. industrial
   e. pastoral

8. According to Part 3 of *Conformity and Conflict*, the relationship of an organism to other elements within its environmental sphere is called
   * a. ecology.
   b. cultural ecology.
   c. the physical environment.
   d. the cultural environment.
   e. biointeraction.

Article 11

The Hunters: Scarce Resources in the Kalahari

RICHARD BORSHAY LEE

With an update by Richard Lee and Megan Biesele

Summary Basing his conclusions on an extensive study of !Kung subsistence activity and nutrition, Richard Lee challenges the notion that hunters and gatherers live a hand-to-mouth existence. Despite residence in the Kalahari Desert, where there is an average yearly rainfall of only six to nine inches, !Kung manage to lead a remarkably stable, relaxed existence. They reside in camps located at permanent water holes. They frequently visit relatives in other camps but rarely move long distances to hunt and gather. A key to assured subsistence is the availability of vegetable foods, particularly the mongongo nut. !Kung can subsist entirely on such foods although they prefer meat. Vegetable foods make up about 75 percent of their diet. The abundance of their sparse environment is revealed by the fact that !Kung eat selectively, consuming only some of the edible plant and animal species found around them. A significant number of !Kung live beyond the age of 60 and approximately 40 percent of the population does no productive work. !Kung spend only about two and one-half days a week in productive activity, using the remainder of their time for leisure activities. Lee concludes that for many hunting and gathering groups, a dependence on plant foods produces a stable, effective way of life.

The way of life described for 1963 has changed, however. By 1994, most Ju/'Hoansi !Kung were living in permanent settlements eking out a living by herding, farming and craft production. Hunting and gathering now only supply about 30 percent of their subsistence needs. The spread of commercial ranching on the areas in which they traditionally foraged may soon reduce this figure to zero.

QUESTIONS

True or False?

T 1.   Richard Lee claims that the consumption of edible plants, rather than meat, was the key to successful subsistence for the !Kung in 1963.

F 2.   Lee found that in 1963, from 60 to 90 percent of the !Kung diet consisted of meat brought back to camp by the men.

T 3.   Despite residence in a sparse desert environment, the !Kung did not eat a majority of the edible plants and animals found in their territory when observed in 1963.

F   4.   Because their environment was so difficult, the !Kung relied heavily on the labor of children and old people to provide edible plants for general consumption in 1963.

T   5.   According to Lee, in 1963 the !Kung have more leisure time than average Americans.

F   6.   One reason the study of !Kung subsistence patterns is so important is the rarity of the case; the !Kung had had no contact with other people until the study began in 1963.

T   7.   Over the 30 years since Lee first described them, the Ju/'Hoansi !Kung have come to live in permanent villages and have become much less dependent on foraging to meet their subsistence needs.

Multiple Choice

1.   According to Richard Lee, in 1963 !Kung men
  * a.   supplied between 20 and 40 percent of the calories consumed by members of a camp.
    b.   hunted almost every day to bag sufficient food for people's daily needs.
    c.   collected approximately 70 percent of the edible vegetable foods.
    d.   began hunting regularly before they are ten years old.
    e.   most often used hunting nets to bag game.

2.   Lee feels that the key to successful subsistence for many hunter-gatherers, such as the !Kung, is
    a.   the presence of large game animals.
    b.   adequate defense against the encroachment of other hunting and gathering groups.
    c.   dietary selectivity.
  * d.   dependence largely on a diet of edible plants.
    e.   band loyalty and membership stability.

3.   According to Lee, the most important staple in the diet of the !Kung when studied in 1963 was
    a.   taro root.
  * b.   the mongongo nut.
    c.   giraffe meat.
    d.   a kind of bitter berry.
    e.   ostrich eggs.

4.   According to Lee and Biesele, by 1994 Ju/'Hoansi !Kung were
  * a.   living in mud-walled houses behind makeshift stockades.
    b.   living in circular, tight-knit villages.
    c.   obtaining about 70 percent of their food through hunting and gathering.
    d.   two of the above.
    e.   a, b, and c above.

5. In his article on the !Kung, Lee claims that when he studied them in the 1960s
   a.   !Kung ate almost all of the edible plants and animals found in their environment.
   b.   lived in camps each of which had a defended territory.
 * c.   enjoyed a large amount of leisure time.
   d.   had to move every few days in search of scarce food stuffs.
   e.   showed clear signs of malnutrition.

6. According to Lee, in 1963 the !Kung had a caloric intake of about _____ per person per day.
   a.   4,000
   b.   3,030
 * c.   2,410
   d.   2,140
   e.   1,890

7. An important point stressed by Lee (The Hunters: Scarce Resources in the Kalahari) about the Ju/'Hoansi !Kung he studied in 1963 was that
   a.   both adults and children had to work every days to insure a sufficient food supply.
   b.   the !Kung had to use virtually all of the edible plants and animals in their environment in order to survive in the desert.
 * c.   life in the state of nature was not necessarily nasty, brutish, and short.
   d.   meat provided more calories in the !Kung diet than other foods.
   e.   none of the above.

8. Four of the following statements about the !Kung as Lee describes their lives in 1963 are true. Which one is **not**?
 * a.   they normally live in a "core area" about 6 miles in circumference
   b.   the proportion of old people to the rest of the population is about the same as that of modern industrial society
   c.   boys and girls usually assume food collecting activities on a regular basis at puberty
   d.   they have much more leisure time than Americans
   e.   none of the above

9. According to Lee and Biesele, in order to survive today, the Ju/'Hoansi Kung will have to
   a.   find new sources of wild foods.
   b.   specialize in the manufacture of trade goods for tourists.
   c.   take jobs in nearby cities in order to earn cash.
 * d.   form borehole syndicates and stake out ranches to protect their foraging areas.
   e.   open reproductions of traditional foraging camps in order to attract tourists.

Article 12

Adaptive Failure: Easter's End   JARAD DIAMOND

Summary In this article, Jarad Diamond argues that ecological degradation ended the civilization on Easter Island and that the forces that were at work there are present throughout the world today. Basing his discussion on historical evidence and on the prehistoric evidence produced by archaeology and the analysis of prehistoric pollen and the remains of animals, he describes how the Polynesians who first discovered the island between 400 and 700 AD found themselves in an abundant land. Pollen analysis indicated that the island was heavily forested by palms and linden trees as well as woody shrubs. The island was also probably the most important breeding ground for sea birds in the South Pacific. Because of its volcanic origin, its soils were rich and ideally suited to grow the Polynesian food plants brought by the first settlers.

Evidence shows that between 700 and 1400 AD, people subsisted on their crops and a surprising number of porpoises, sea birds, land birds, and rats, the latter having hitched a ride to the island in their canoes. Fish were also a source of food but of less importance. The Easter Island population rose to 7000 during this period and clans began to quarry, carve, and erect the island's famous "heads." The work required the use of trees as rollers to move the heavy carvings from the quarry to their final destination, and inhabitants eventually used up all the timber on the island for this purpose. By 1400 AD, they no longer had the materials to build canoes, so they could no longer go out to sea to hunt porpoises and fish. They compensated for the loss by raising more chickens and by eating fellow islanders. In 1722, a Dutch captain, Jacob Roggeveen, encountered the island and described it as barren and inhabited by less than 2,000 people. Military leaders had replaced clan chiefs as leaders, and conflict and cannibalism were rife. Subsequent centuries saw a nearly total social collapse on the island. Diamond concludes that islanders failed to see that they were destroying their environment because deterioration occurred so slowly and because social concerns outweighed conservation. By the time they realized what was happening, it was too late.

For Diamond, Easter Island represents a miniature example of what is happening to the world today. People are using up fossil fuels, sea animals, rain forests, and soil at an alarming rate. A difference exists, however, which provides hope for the survival of the modern world. Today, people can record history and see the changes in their environment. They can document cases such as Easter Island and use them to promote conservation.

QUESTIONS

True or False?

F 1. According to Diamond (Adaptive Failure: Easter's End), civilization died out on Easter Island because the Polynesians who arrived there in about 400 to 700 AD did not have the proper technology to exploit the island's natural resources.

T 2. According to Diamond (Adaptive Failure: Easter's End), the history of Polynesian habitation on Easter Island represents a miniature example of what could happen to people everywhere on earth.

F 3. Diamond, citing archaeological evidence, notes that in the early years (700 to 1200 AD) of habitation on Eastern Island by Polynesians, the chief foods eaten by people were fish and oil palm nuts.

T 4. According to Diamond, when Polynesians first reached Eastern Island sometime between 400 and 700 AD, the island was covered by an abundant subtropical forest and was probably the most important breeding ground for sea birds in Polynesia.

F 5. According to Diamond, Easter Islanders turned to eating porpoises and sea birds after 1400 AD when they had exhausted the island's other natural resources.

T 6. Diamond argues that Easter Islanders failed to see that they were destroying their island habitat until it was too late because the changes occurred too slowly to be appreciated by each generation of people and because there was no way to record what the island had been like in the past.

Multiple Choice

1. According to Diamond (Adaptive Failure: Easter's End), the history of human habitation on Easter Island
   a. is an example of what can happen if military leaders take over from civil authorities.
   * b. is a miniature example of what is happening or can happen to earth today.
   c. clearly demonstrates the theories of Erich Von Däniken and Thor Heyerdahl.
   d. shows that some environments are too difficult for people to live in.
   e. none of the above.

2. According to Diamond, a key to preventing what happened on Easter Island from happening to the whole earth is
   a. more efficient technology.
   b. political control of private enterprise.
 * c. the generation and use of information.
   d. an effort by the United Nations to control environmental degradation.
   e. more concerted activity by non governmental organizations such as the Sierra Club.

3. According to Diamond (Easter's End), world populations are using up four of the following resources faster than they can be replaced. Which one is **not** a resource they are using up?
 * a. solar energy
   b. rain forests
   c. fossil fuels
   d. fish and other sea animals used for food
   e. soil

4. According to Diamond (Easter's End), during the early period of human habitation on Easter Island (700 to 1200 AD), _____ were the most common source of animal protein.
   a. chickens
   b. fish
   c. land birds
 * d. porpoises
   e. sea snails.

5. According to Diamond (Easter's End), Easter Islanders failed to prevent the destruction of their island's natural resources because
   a. changes in the environment occurred too slowly for succeeding generations to notice.
   b. social and biological requirements outweighed the need to conserve.
   c. clan chiefs sought to enrich themselves by collecting and selling natural products.
 * d. two of the above.
   e. a, b, and c above.

6. According to Diamond, Roggeveen, the first European to discover Easter Island, described the island as
   a. volcanic.
   b. overpopulated.
   c. uninhabited.
   d. heavily forested.
 * e. a wasteland.

7. According to Diamond (Easter's End), researchers Flenley and King were able to reconstruct a profile of Easter Island's prehistoric vegetation largely by
   * a. recovering and analyzing prehistoric pollen.
   b. recovering fossilized plants.
   c. analyzing the language of current Easter Islanders for vocabulary naming plants that have since disappeared from the island.
   d. two of the above.
   e. a, b, and c above.

8. According to Diamond, in 1400 AD when the inhabitants of Easter Island ran out of the animals they had been subsisting on since about 700 AD, they turned to eating
   a. sea birds.
   b. porpoises.
   * c. people.
   d. two of the above.
   e. a, b, and c above.

Article 13

Cultivating the Tropical Forest   RICHARD K. REED

Summary Richard Reed discusses the human use of the Amazonian tropical forest in this article about the Guarani of Paraguay. He points out that there has been growing concern over the destruction of tropical forests, but little understanding of how indigenous peoples live in them or how such peoples can provide a model for realistic forest policy.

Reed focuses on the Guarani village of Itanarami. Villagers employ a slash-and-burn agriculture technique with a 20-year field rotation cycle. They also rely heavily on hunting, fishing, and foraging for sustenance and for products to sell for money. Above all, he argues, Guarani subsistence practices are designed to permit forest recovery.

Recent development has cleared the forests for soybean farms and cattle ranches. Deprived of land for foraging, Guarani must now grow more crops to eat and sell. The forest no longer renews itself and many Indians have become landless peasant laborers.

Recently, the government has established a "biosphere reserve" that will permit some Guarani to continue their traditional forest exploitation. In the long run, planners believe the land will produce more value this way than if it were commercially developed for farming or ranching.

QUESTIONS

True or False?

T   1.   According to Reed (Cultivating the Tropical Forest), the Guarani, and in the past, millions of Indians, exploited the Amazonian tropical forests without causing permanent harm to the ecosystem.

F   2.   Reed claims that the single key to successful subsistence in the Amazon tropical forest is slash-and-burn agriculture.

T   3.   The Guarani, according to Reed, exploit the forest commercially as well as for subsistence.

F   4.   Reed argues that people must be prevented from living in the Amazon forest if the tropical ecosystem is to survive.

T   5.   According to Reed, when colonists develop the tropical forest in which Guarani live, the Indians must farm more and more land to survive.

Multiple Choice

1. In his article "Cultivating the Tropical Forest," Reed argues
   a. against the use of the Amazon tropical forest by people.
   b. for government control of forest development that eases the Indians into the modern world economy.
   * c. for human forest exploitation using slash-and-burn and foraging technologies.
   d. for an Indian relocation plan.
   e. for government aid to support Indians displaced by modern forest development.

2. According to Reed, Guarani Indians subsist in the Amazon tropical forest largely by
   a. slash-and-burn farming.
   * b. horticulture and foraging.
   c. foraging.
   d. cattle ranching.
   e. rubber tree tapping.

3. Which one of the following was **not** a consequence of outside development in the Guarani tropical forests, according to Reed?
   * a. the Indians who stayed on the land could no longer farm
   b. the Guarani could no longer practice horticulture
   c. disease and malnutrition increased
   d. the Indians could no longer forage
   e. men often left for work on ranches or commercial farms

4. Reed argues that, for the Guarani, _____ was essential to subsistence.
   a. farming
   b. foraging
   c. the combination of rubber tree tapping and foraging
   d. the combination of hunting and gathering
   * e. the combination of farming and foraging

5. According to Reed, the Amazon tropical forest
   a. cannot sustain farming.
   b. can be developed for farming with the use of pesticides.
   c. can be used for ranching in special "biosphere reserves."
   * d. can support human populations that practice field and foraging rotation.
   e. can be used for lumbering with a forest rotation and replanting program.

Article 14

Domestication and the Evolution of Disease **JARAD DIAMOND**

Summary In this article written to commemorate the 500 year anniversary of Columbus' arrival in the Americans. Jarad Diamond traces the evolution and impact of old world "crowd diseases" that not only regularly devastated European populations but also killed about 95 percent of the Indians of the Americas. Originally affecting only domesticated animals and those, such as rats and chickens that live close to people, diseases such as smallpox, flu, measles, plague, cholera, and chicken pox evolved to afflict their human keepers. Since these epidemic diseases were originally unknown in the new world, they ravaged American Indian populations who lacked any resistance to them. Because the necessary conditions for the development of crowd diseases were absent in the new world, there were few diseases to spread from the Americas to Europe and Asia.

Diamond identifies two kinds of diseases based on how they are spread: passive and active. Passive diseases move from one host to another through intermediaries such as insects, or when their flesh is eaten. Malaria and trichinosis are examples. Active diseases cause hosts to infect others. The running sores caused by syphilis and smallpox, the coughs and sneezing that accompany colds and whooping cough, or the diarrhea caused by cholera, are examples.

The human body responds to diseases by trying to kill off or limit the reproduction of the microbes that cause them. Fevers and the actions of white cells and antibodies represent human responses. But germs fight back by producing new antigens or, like AIDS, evolving them steadily. Over time people also develop genes that help them resist diseases and gain partial immunity.

The attributes of epidemic diseases include rapid exposure, a kill or cure outcome, survivors with antibodies that give lasting immunity, and the presence of large sedentary human populations. Travel and trade aid in the spread of infectious diseases.

Most epidemic diseases have emerged as mutations of animal diseases that are not able to attack humans. Infectious diseases evolve from those afflicting animals to full blown human plagues in four stages. First is a stage where some people are infected by a disease but can't spread it to each other. Catscratch fever and psitacosis are examples. Second, diseases may evolve to be spread from one person to another but die out once they have infected a human population. O'nyong nyong spread from monkeys to humans in Africa in 1959 but disappeared once it had run its course. Third, some diseases, such as Lyme disease and Lassa fever evolve to infect humans but do not die out. They remain a constant threat to human populations. Finally, some diseases infect humans in pulses, killing and reappearing. These are the crowd diseases. If they are around long enough, however, they may evolve less lethal strains so that they don't kill themselves by killing their hosts. Syphilis killed its victims rapidly when it first appeared in 1495 but by 1546 produced a lingering death.

It was the crowd diseases, evolved in the old world among large human populations that lived in close association with domesticated animals and animal pests, which killed the Indians of the Americas. For example, smallpox, which arrived in 1524, killed half the people of Mexico City, the rulers of the Inca Empire, and many of the mound builders living in the Mississippi valley within a few short decades. With no resistance, Indians died by the millions and their societies collapsed, opening the way for European conquest. Without herd animals to domesticate and large urban centers connected by trade, new infectious diseases did not evolve in the Americas and afflict the old world invaders.

QUESTIONS

True or False?

T 1. Jarad Diamond (Domestication and the Evolution of Disease) argues that crowd diseases such as smallpox evolved in the old world because of population growth and high density, the domestication of animals, and the advent of extensive trade.

F 2. According to Diamond, infectious diseases appeared when humans contacted remote areas of the world where only animals harbored the troublesome microbes.

F 3. According to Diamond, malaria is an active diseases whereas syphilis is a passive disease.

T 4. Diamond classifies diseases into active and passive types on the basis of whether or not the disease organisms cause the host to provide a way to spread the microbes to others.

T 5. Attributes of infectious diseases include rapid exposure, an outcome marked by death or a complete cure, and lasting antibodies among survivors.

F 6. Hunter/gatherers provided an ideal population within which crowd diseases, such as smallpox, could evolve and spread.

T 7. Indians of the Americas failed to evolve crowd diseases because they had few domesticated animals and lacked significant trade between cities.

F 8. Symptoms, such as coughs and diarrhea are the human body's way of fighting diseases according to Diamond.

Multiple Choice

1. According to Diamond (Domestication and the Evolution of Disease), most epidemic diseases
   a. evolved in the Americas but failed to spread because populations were too small there.
 * b. evolved in the old world as a result of growing sedentary human populations and the domestication of animals.
   c. evolved in Africa from diseases that afflicted monkeys and great apes, the nearest human relatives.
   d. evolved in Asia where they are closely associated with vectors such as the Asian tiger mosquito.
   e. are tropical in origin.

2. According to Diamond, active diseases are those which
 * a. cause their hosts to spread them through such means as open sores and coughs.
   b. diseases whose presence can actually be seen by looking for symptoms.
   c. diseases that kill their hosts as opposed to passive diseases that may linger on for years.
   d. diseases that destroy the cells of hosts rather than simply inhabiting them.
   e. diseases that reproduce in hosts rather than lying dormant in them.

3. According to Diamond (Domestication and the Evolution of Disease), the attributes of epidemic diseases include
   a. steady continual infection of small populations.
   b. steady continual infections of large compact populations.
 * c. the production of survivors who have long-lasting antibodies.
   d. the infection of a large number of people with slow-acting, lingering symptoms.
   e. none of the above.

4. Diamond (Domestication and the Evolution of Disease) argues that four of the following are attributes of epidemic diseases. Which one is **not**?
   a. they enjoy a rapid exposure
   b. they kill a high percentage of their victims but those who survive have lasting immunity
 * c. they tend to afflict human populations in a steady, persistent manner
   d. they leave survivors with antibodies that last (lasting immunity)
   e. they are associated with large, dense populations

5. Diamond (Domestication and the Evolution of Disease) classifies human diseases into active and passive. Which one of the following is a passive disease based on Diamond's examples?
   a. plague
   b. measles
   c. cholera
 * d. malaria
   e. influenza

6. According to Diamond (Domestication and the Evolution of Disease), the pulses (periods of infection in a population followed by many disease-free years) that are characteristic of epidemic diseases are primarily caused by the fact that
   a. the diseases attenuate themselves because if they kill their hosts they kill themselves.
   b. disease organisms "grow tired" much as human cells do as a person ages, and eventually die off.
   c. the entire human population dies so the disease can't find any more victims.
   d. human medical (cultural) responses such as the development of antibiotics can stop infection for long periods of time.
 * e. survivors have immunity for life so new epidemics can only start with the birth and accumulation of new society members who lack immunity.

7. Diamond (Domestication and the Evolution of Disease) argues that hunter/gatherers were not afflicted by epidemic diseases because
   a. their populations were too small.
   b. they moved their camps several times a year, which contributed to good sanitation.
   c. they did not keep domesticated animals, the primary source of infectious diseases.
   d. they did not engage in long-distance trading on a regular basis.
 * e. all of the above.

8. Diamond (Domestication and the Evolution of Disease) explains the absence of epidemic diseases among the peoples of the Americas by noting that new world peoples lacked
   a. domesticated animals, the source of most infectious diseases.
   b. cities with unsanitary conditions.
   c. cities and states connected by regular trade.
 * d. two of the above.
   e. a, b, and c above.

9. According to Diamond (Domestication and the Evolution of Disease), old world crowd diseases killed _____ percent of the Indians of the Americas in the first 100 years after Columbus' arrival in the new world.
 * a. 95
   b. 80
   c. 70
   d. 50
   e. 30

PART 4

ECONOMY AND GLOBALIZATION

The introduction to Part 4 discusses the basic elements of the economic system including types of exchange.

KEY DEFINITIONS

The **economic system** refers to the provision of goods and services to meet biological and social wants.

Production refers to the process of rendering material items useful and available for human consumption.

Allocation of resources refers to the cultural rules people use to assign rights to ownership and use of resources.

Technology is the cultural knowledge for making and using tools and extracting and refining raw materials.

The **division of labor** refers to the rules that govern the assignment of jobs to people.

Unit of production defines the persons or groups responsible for producing goods and services.

Market exchange is the transfer of goods and services based on price, supply, and demand.

Reciprocal exchange is the transfer of goods services between two people or groups based on role obligation.

Redistribution refers to the transfer of goods and services between a central collecting source and a group of individuals.

QUESTIONS

True or False?

T   1.   A good example of reciprocal exchange in American society is gift giving at birthdays.

F   2.   Division of labor refers to the person or organized group responsible for producing something.

F   3.   When people buy and sell goods and services on the basis of price, supply, and demand, we call the process redistributive exchange.

T   4.   Market exchange is associated with many larger societies where people must be able to procure a wide variety of goods and services from strangers.

F   5.   Because they are based on role obligations, taxes are an example of reciprocal exchange.

T   6.   The economic system defines the provision of goods and services to meet human biological and social wants.

F   7.   Technology refers to the machines people use to make things.

Multiple Choice

1.   The provision of goods and services to meet biological and social wants is called
    a.   production.
* b.   the economic system.
    c.   market exchange.
    d.   division of labor.
    e.   he unit of production.

2.   One would expect to find the least job specialization in a
* a.   hunting and gathering society.
    b.   horticultural society.
    c.   industrial society.
    d.   agricultural society.
    e.   pastoral society.

3.   The cultural knowledge for making and using tools and extracting and refining raw materials is called
    a.   production.
    b.   division of labor.
    c.   unit of production.
* d.   technology.
    e.   economic plans.

4. Gift giving among family members at Christmas is an example of
   a. allocation of resources.
   b. market exchange.
 * c. reciprocal exchange.
   d. redistributive exchange.
   e. barter.

5. Taxes would best be classified as a form of
   a. barter.
   b. allocation of resources.
   c. market exchange.
   d. reciprocal exchange.
 * e. redistributive exchange.

Article 15

Reciprocity and the Power of Giving

LEE CRONK

Summary In this article, Cronk discusses the nature and functions of gift giving, using examples from many societies including our own. He introduces the topic by describing two historical cases of gift exchange between North American Indians and U.S. colonists, noting the importance of gift giving to the former. He argues that everywhere in the world, gifts are used positively to establish and maintain social relationships, but also negatively to intimidate and fight others. These characteristics apply just as fully to gift exchange in industrial societies as they do for other peoples.

Anthropologists learned about the complexities of gift giving through first-hand experience during fieldwork. Richard Lee's !Kung informants criticized his gift of an ox, saying the ox was thin and inadequate when clearly it was not. (See article 2 in *Conformity and Conflict*). Rada Dyson-Hudson met with a similar reaction when she attempted to give pots to her Turkana informants. Cronk also experienced the same reaction when he gave clothing to the Mukogodo, who elaborate the act of gift exchange more than do most people. In every case, informants attached different meanings to gift giving than did the anthropologists, and reacted in unexpected ways.

Gift giving has several dimensions, including how the gift is received and how it is reciprocated. Often "to reciprocate at once indicates a desire to end the relationship," Cronk points out. He also notes that some gift giving arrangements, such as *hxaro* among the !Kung, are designed solely to maintain a friendly relationship. In addition, the worth of gifts may not be taken into account. The Trobriand *kula* ring, involving shell necklaces and arm bands, represents one of the most elaborate gift exchanges ever described by anthropologists.

Gift giving may not always be benevolent. The Kwakiutl *potlatch*, where rivals tried to "flatten" each other with gifts, is a good example. Potlatching actually became a substitute for war after the Canadian government suppressed real fighting.

Reciprocal gift giving is also important in U.S. society. For example, anthropologist Carol Stack found a form of benevolent gift giving, called *swapping* among African Americans living in an area of Illinois called the flats. Sociologist Warren Hagstrom points out that scientific papers, usually referred to as *contributions*, are really gifts and have higher value than those papers written for money. Even the citations of other people's work so liberally scattered throughout academic papers may be viewed as a form of gift exchange.

Gifts may also be used to manipulate people, as Grace Goodell documents for a World Bank-funded project in Iran. The gift of an irrigation project crushed local level political organizations and shifted control to the central government.

International relations often involve gift giving. The "concessions" made between the US and Soviet governments during disarmament negotiations several years ago are a good example.

Cronk concludes by pointing out that American Indians understood the gift's power to unify, antagonize, or subjugate and that all of us would do well to learn the same lesson.

QUESTIONS

True or False?

T 1. According to Cronk in his article, "Reciprocity and the Power of Giving," gift giving can be used to intimidate people.

F 2. Cronk (Reciprocity and the Power of Giving) argues that in most instances of gift giving, donors expect those who have received the gift to reciprocate promptly.

T 3. Cronk (Reciprocity and the Power of Giving) argues that citations of other people's work in academic articles as well as the articles themselves, are a form of gift.

F 4. According to Cronk, the phrase "Indian giver" arose because North American Indians misunderstood European customs and wanted gifts they gave to colonists to be returned promptly and with interest.

F 5. Cronk reports that no matter how little he gave his Mukogodo informants while he was doing fieldwork, they always seemed grateful, which led to a warmer, more trusting relationship demonstrating the positive power of giving.

T 6. Cronk argues that gift giving is an important way for people to initiate and maintain relationships in every society.

Multiple Choice

1. According to Cronk in his article, "Reciprocity and the Power of Giving," people use gift giving to
    a. initiate relationships.
    b. maintain relationships.
    c. fight.
    d. two of the above.
  * e. a, b, and c above

2. According to Cronk, the Kwakiutl *potlatch* is a good example of a way to
   a. establish friendly alliances, in this case between clans.
   b. maintain equal social relationships between different clan members.
   * c. fight or flatten social rivals.
   d. establish alliances between competing political factions.
   e. create future material wealth for the giver.

3. Cronk, citing work by sociologist Warren Hagstrom, argues that _____ represent gifts in a system of reciprocal exchange.
   * a. citations in academic articles
   b. food
   c. business lunches
   d. alcoholic drinks
   e. blankets, coppers, and arm shells

4. Cronk notes that four of the following are good examples of reciprocal gift giving. Which one is **not**?
   a. academic articles submitted to academic journals
   * b. shoes bought at a local mall
   c. concessions made between U.S. and Russian negotiators during peace negotiations a few years ago
   d. shell necklaces and arm bands traded in ritual fashion in the Trobriand Island exchange system called the *kula*
   e. "swapping" reported by Carol Stack for African Americans living in a place in Illinois called the flats

5. Cronk, reporting on a study by Grace Goodell, notes that monetary support of an irrigation project by the _____ served to _____ in Iran.
   a. U.S.:   support local level political organizations
   b. World Bank: support local level political organizations
   c. U.S.:   crush local level political organizations
   * d. World Bank: crush local level political organizations
   e. U.S.:   revive local level political organizations

6. According to Cronk, which one of the following is a clear example of gift giving designed to "flatten" someone else with generosity?
   a. Richard Lee's gift of a Christmas ox to the !Kung with whom he did fieldwork in the Kalahari desert
   b. "concessions" made by U.S. and Russian peace negotiators
   c. "swapping" among African Americans living in a place called the flats
   d. the Trobriand *kula* ring
   * e. the Kwakiutl *potlatch*

Article 16

Cocaine and the Economic Deterioration of Bolivia

JACK McIVER WEATHERFORD

Summary This article by Jack Weatherford points out the devastation the Western appetite for cocaine has wreaked on the people of rural Bolivia. It might be easy to think that the cocaine trade, damaging as it is to Western society, might at least benefit a poor country such as Bolivia, which produces the drug. In fact, some urban Bolivians show signs of wealth derived from trading cocaine. Just as certainly, however, cocaine has seriously damaged the rural social structure and economy of the country. Men have left the villages to work in cocaine processing and transportation. They send little or nothing home, begin to depend on the drug themselves, and may become angry exploiters of their own kin. Only women and children are left to work the potato fields. Cocaine has replaced potatoes and other foods as the main cargo on the few trucks that serve the country. Potatoes are scarce in some areas and piled up unsold in others as a result. In addition, the cocaine trade has contributed to a run-away inflation, displaced hunter-gatherers whose forest lands are being cleared for coca plantations, and severely damaged the health of the men, women, and children who work in the production and transport of coca leaves and cocaine. American pressure on Bolivia to do something about the cocaine trade hurts largely the small farmers who grow coca leaves, and some of the poor people who work to produce cocaine.

QUESTIONS

True or False?

F 1. In this article on Bolivia, Weatherford shows how cocaine production has broken down class distinctions in the countryside.

T 2. Weatherford argues that the world market for cocaine has had just as damaging an effect on the Bolivian economy as it has on the users it supplies.

F 3. One effect that cocaine production has had on villages like Pocona is to increase demand for agricultural produce to feed workers, thus causing shortages back home.

T 4. *Pistococas* are people who tread on a mixture of kerosene, and coca leaves.

F 5. The demand for coca leaves has driven many farmers into the lowland rain forest to grow potatoes.

T 6. According to Weatherford, the cocaine trade has disrupted the Bolivian transportation system.

Multiple Choice

1. In his article on the impact of the market for cocaine on the Bolivian economy, Weatherford argues that
    a. cocaine, while damaging its users, has been a blessing to Bolivian farmers.
    b. the cocaine trade is providing the capital necessary for Bolivian development.
    * c. the cocaine trade has disrupted the traditional rural Bolivian economy.
    d. two of the above.
    e. none of the above.

2. According to Weatherford, which one of the following is an effect of the cocaine trade on the Bolivian economy?
    a. it threatens to displace lowland hunter-gatherers
    b. it contributes to national inflation
    c. is has increased the rural production of *chica*
    d. two of the above
    * e. a, b, and c above

3. Four of the following are effects of the international market for cocaine on Bolivians, according to Weatherford. Which one is **not**?
    a. it has reduced calcium intake
    * b. it has increased potato production for export to cities
    c. it has contributed to inflation
    d. it has caused the feet of *pistacocas* (cocaine workers) to ulcerate
    e. it has disrupted family life

4. The chewing of coca leaves, according to Weatherford, does **not**
    * a. cause intoxication.
    b. increase calcium intake.
    c. reduce the pain of headache.
    d. reduce hunger pangs.
    e. treat *sorroche*.

5. According to Weatherford, one young man who traveled to the Chapare to work in cocaine production
    a. sent home most of his money.
    * b. eventually took his ten-year-old sister to be a servant so he could make more money.
    c. supplied his family with cocaine.
    d. two of the above.
    e. none of the above.

6. According to Weatherford, Bolivian villagers are going hungry in the mountains because
   a. they all chew the more available coca leaves instead of keeping them for sale.
 * b. men have gone to the Chapare to work in cocaine production.
   c. villagers are shipping all their food to cities where the demand to feed cocaine workers is high.
   d. two of the above.
   e. a, b, and c above.

Article 17

Workaday World—Crack Economy

PHILIPPE BOURGOIS

Summary In this article, Philippe Bourgois describes the work done by young Latino and African American crack dealers in New York where higher paying manufacturing jobs have disappeared.

Bourgois, who first went to live in Harlem with his wife in 1985, intended to study the underground (untaxed) economy there. He discovered that about a third of the women who lived in Harlem received public assistance and that many augmented their meager checks with side work, such as baby sitting, bartending in after hours clubs, and sewing. They also often received support from amorous relationships with men who made cash contributions to their household expenses. Male income strategies were more public, and included curb-side car repair, unlicensed construction, and running numbers (a betting game). Within a short time after his arrival, however, crack cocaine appeared on the market and many men began to sell the drug. Bourgois also discovered that a large number of Harlem residents held taxable, near minimum wage, jobs—48 percent for men and 35 percent for women over 16 for the city, 53 percent for men and 28 percent for women in the part of Harlem where he lived. He asks why men would work in the formal economy for low pay when more money can be had selling crack? Conversely, if official work is more popular, why do so many men sell crack?

The answer to the first question lies in the nature of selling crack. Bourgois describes the life of a dealer named Primo. Primo works in a crack house, a broken down store front with a few arcade games, poor lighting, and no toilet. He is bothered by the "fucked up" addicts he sees every day. And worse, his percentage of the daily income is only about twice the minimum wage. Primo actually wants legal work; the money he earns from selling crack is higher, but he hates the job. Why, then, doesn't he get a job in the formal economy?

The answer emerges when we look at a structural change in the New York City job market. Over the last 45 years, the number of jobs has remained the same at about 3,500,000, but factory jobs, which paid enough to support a family and which were open to unskilled labor, have been replaced by service jobs in the "FIRE" economy. FIRE stands for finance, insurance, and real-estate companies. These companies offer men like Primo minimum wage jobs as mail clerks, messengers, and photocopiers. Males on the street are not socialized to accept the public subordination that goes along with these low status jobs, nor the degradation that comes from lack of education when they can't read notes or "fail to follow directions." They feel disrespected. Hence, selling crack is often a more viable, if distasteful, occupation. Bourgois ends with the story of how Primo dropped out of a motivational group program designed to help men like him get regular jobs because he lacked a dress shirt to wear to class and felt "like a bum."

QUESTIONS

True or False?

F 1. According to Bourgois, Latino and African American residents of Harlem have often turned to selling crack cocaine because they can't find work in New York City.

F 2. In his article on the Latino and African American men who sell crack cocaine in Harlem, Bourgois notes that only 25 percent of male Harlem residents work in "official" jobs.

T 3. Bourgois notes that most Harlem men have at one time or another held official jobs in New York City's service economy.

F 4. According to Bourgois, the FIRE economy that characterizes the New York City labor market largely consists of dirty sweatshop manufacturing jobs.

T 5. Bourgois argues that Harlem men feel degraded and disrespected in the entry level service jobs they can get at insurance, real-estate, and financial companies.

Multiple Choice

1. Bourgois (Workaday World—Crack Economy) argues that men from Harlem don't find it easy to work for New York City's service industries because
   a. these pay too little.
 * b. the men feel they are treated with disrespect in such industries.
   c. they are not physically strong enough to work at such jobs.
   d. two of the above.
   e. none of the above.

2. According to Bourgois, the New York City FIRE economy means service jobs in
 * a. the insurance, real estate, and finance industries.
   b. liability insurance firms.
   c. government offices.
   d. telemarketing.
   e. fundamental recycling firms.

3. According to Bourgois, his friend and informant, Primo, does not like dealing crack cocaine because
   a. he resents working for crack suppliers.
   b. he is disgusted by the behavior of the addicts he must so often sell to.
   c. he does not like the terrible conditions under which he has to work.
 * d. two of the above.
   e. a, c, and c above.

61

4. According to Bourgois (Workaday World—Crack Economy), the New York City economy
    a. has lost thousands of jobs since 1950.
    b. is dominated by manufacturing jobs requiring unskilled labor.
    * c. has the same number of jobs that it did in 1950 but more of these are in the service industry.
    d. only has jobs that can be held by educated people.
    e. none of the above.

5. According to Bourgois, Harlem crack dealers such as Primo
    a. only make minimum wage when all the time they spend at this job is taken into account.
    b. regularly make a $100 or more an hour.
    * c. make about double the U.S. minimum hourly wage.
    d. must turn over one-third of what they make to their suppliers who also often own the crack houses.
    e. none of the above.

6. According to Bourgois (Workaday World—Crack Economy),
    a. 78 percent of the women in Harlem receive public assistance.
    * b. 53 percent of the Harlem men in his census were working at taxable jobs.
    c. over half the Latino and African American men in Harlem sell crack cocaine because of the high living standard the money they make affords them.
    d. the only jobs Latino and African American men can get in Harlem are dirty manufacturing jobs.
    e. none of the above.

7. According to Bourgois, his informant, Primo, dropped out of a motivational group program designed to help him enter the legitimate job world because
    a. he was ashamed of the fact that he couldn't read.
    b. he did not think the program would help him.
    c. the program was run by women.
    d. he did not like the jobs the program was preparing him for.
    * e. he lacked nice enough clothes to wear in the class.

8. A point made by Bourgois in his article, "Workaday World—Crack Economy," is that
    a. a change from factory to service jobs in the New York City labor market has made it hard for men in Harlem to find a regular job that pays a living wage.
    b. New York City jobs in the FIRE economy make Harlem men feel disrespected.
    c. most men want to work at legal, taxable, jobs.
    d. two of the above.
    * e. a, b, and c above.

Article 18

Illegal Logging and Frontier Conservation

NATHAN WILLIAMSON

Summary This article by Nathan Williamson discusses the complex problems that arise when policies based on good intensions meet the economic necessities of daily life. Alarmed by the commercial destruction of the world's tropical forests, several non-governmental organizations (NGOs) as well as some governments, have launched conservation programs largely designed to promote sustainable forest exploitation. As Williamson shows here, this was the case for Bolivia when Conservation International engaged in a debt for nature swap with the Bolivian government to set up a biosphere reserve that included the Chimanes forest in Beni Department. With the participation of the International Tropical Timber Organization, seven companies were licensed to cut timber in the Chimanes forest using sustainable methods. But as Williamson discovered, the realities of life on this Amazonian frontier paint a different picture, one marked the illegal logging of Chimanes Indians and small-scale entrepreneurs, and evasion of the rules by commercial logging companies. Williamson shows how the economic necessities of life on the frontier have encouraged Chimanes Indians to illegally cut and market mahogany from their forest, which was off limits to exploitation. In addition, the Indians help *cuartoneros* (chainsaw crews) to find and illegally cut mahogany and other hardwoods. Although their work is unbelievably difficult, *cuartoneros* are also attracted to the forest by higher wages in a part of Bolivia where work is scarce and wages appallingly low. A system has emerged to handle illegally cut wood. The Chimanes and *cuartoneros* sell their illegal wood to small-scale timber buyers or lumber mill owners. From there, the wood is often bought by commercial lumber companies which claim it was legally cut. They ship the timber to the highlands where some of it is exported to foreign countries. In addition, the commercial logging companies often cut timber in unsustainable ways in violation of the initial agreements. Thus, economic necessity, the high demand for tropical hardwoods, and the inability of the Bolivian government to enforce it policies on what is largely a lawless frontier (readers might look at the history of the conditions on the North American frontier for a similar case) have thwarted well-meaning conservation policies. Williamson concludes that only international limitations on the sale of tropical hardwoods or a program that permits small-scale logging, which is far less destructive than commercial logging, combined with replanting can save the forest.

QUESTIONS

True or False?

T   1.   According to Nathan Williamson (Illegal Logging and Frontier Conservation), Bolivian government plans to create a biosphere reserve in the Chamanes forest have failed to work because of the economic necessities facing the colonists and Chimanes Indians who live there, the inability of the Bolivian government to control the frontier, and the evasive practices of commercial logging companies.

F   2.   According to Williamson (Illegal Logging and Frontier Conservation), the culture of the Chimanes Indians living in the Bolivian Amazon has been largely destroyed by the illegal practices of commercial logging companies

T   3.   According to Williamson (Illegal Logging and Frontier Conservation), the most effective way Chimanes Indians can make money to meet such expenses as their need to buy tools and their children's school supplies is by illegally cutting and selling tropical hardwoods from their forest preserve.

F   4.   Williamson (Illegal Logging and Frontier Conservation), argues that the Bolivian government is secretly behind the illegal logging that goes on in the eastern lowlands Chimanes forest.

T   5.   According to Williamson (Illegal Logging and Frontier Conservation), the logging by *cuartoneros* (chainsaw gangs) in the Chimanes forest of Bolivia is less destructive to the forest than selective cutting by commercial companies.

F   6.   According to Williamson (Illegal Logging and Frontier Conservation), commercial loggers licensed to conduct sustainable logging in Bolivia's Chimanes forest have tried to suppress the illegal logging of *cuartoneros* (chainsaw gangs) and Chinames Indians.

Multiple Choice

1.   According to Nathan Williamson (Illegal Logging and Frontier Conservation), programs for sustainable logging in Bolivia's Chimanes Forest have largely failed because of
   a.   the resistance of Chimanes Indians who wish to continue their destructive practice of slash and burn agriculture.
   * b.   the attraction of money made from illegal logging to Chimanes Indians and frontier colonists and the high price of tropical hardwoods on the international market.
   c.   corrupt Bolivian Governmental officials who control illegal logging operations and have made a fortune from international sales.
   d.   the fact that there is no possible way to log the Chimanes forest in a sustainable way.
   e.   the desire of Bolivian colonists who have flooded into the area to clear the land for ranching and farming.

2. Williamson (Illegal Logging and Frontier Conservation), *cuartoneros* are
   a. Chimanes Indians who illegally log their government-provided forest preserve.
   b. small-scale timber buyers living in San Borja who sell illegal lumber to larger commercial timber companies
   * c. chainsaw gang members who illegally cut selected hardwoods in the Chimanes forest.
   d. Bolivian government officials who must be bribed in order for logging companies to illegally cut trees in the Chimanes forest preserve.
   e. roving bands of poor colonists who steal timber from Chimanes Indians and loot their villages.

3. According to Williamson (Illegal Logging and Frontier Conservation), the Campero family described in the article could make about _____ after expenses from selling a raft load of wood in San Borja, Bolivia.
   a. $1000
   b. $530
   c. $400
   * d. $220
   e. $160

4. Williamson (Illegal Logging and Frontier Conservation) notes that an NGO, Conservation International, arranged a debt-for-nature swap with the Bolivian government in order to establish a
   a. forest preserve in the Chimanes forest that would be free of logging.
   b. biosphere preserve free of logging that could still be open for tourists.
   c. forest preserve set aside for Chimanes Indians that would permit the Chimanes to log in a sustainable manner and sell the timber to the Bolivian government.
   * d. forest preserve that could be logged in a sustainable manner by commercial logging companies.
   e. none of the above

5. According to Williamson (Illegal Logging and Frontier Conservation), it is difficult for mahogany trees to reforest an area once they are cut because
   a. forest underbrush smothers the young saplings.
   b. they only produce seeds every four or five years.
   * c. only large mature trees produce seeds and these are the ones loggers cut.
   d. heavy tropical rains wash away all the nutrients where the trees once grew so saplings cannot survive.
   e. they can only exist in groves with other mahogany trees and these are destroyed by logging.

6. According to Williamson (Illegal Logging and Frontier Conservation), tropical forests may only be saved by
   a. strict laws against illegal logging.
   b. the establishment or industry and other moneymaking plans in frontier towns like San Borja.
   c. sustainable logging programs such as those promoted by the International Tropical Timber Organization.
   d. the granting of cutting rights only to indigenous peoples such as the Chimanes Indians who know how to preserve the forest.
   * e. by decreasing the world demand for tropical hardwoods by setting importation limits or promoting the sale only of sustainably cut trees.

Article 19

How Sushi Went Global   THEODORE C. BESTOR

Summary This article by Theodore Bestor reveals the complex network of relationships that define a global economic system. Focusing on shushi, a traditional Japanese cuisine, Bestor shows how the international adoption of the culinary custom, and especially its center piece, raw bluefin tuna, has created a global system that involves Atlantic fishing and fish farming, national and environmental regulations, realignments of labor and capital, and shifting markets.

The article begins with a description of a bluefin auction at a fishing pier near Bath main. About 20 buyers evaluate and bid on three large bluefins, consulting buyers in Tsukiui fish market in Japan by cell phone to establish prices. Once bought, the fish are packed in ice and flown to Japan. Japanese have a long-term affection for the bluefin, a fish that was originally caught only for sport in the U.S. The Japanese turned to foreign tuna suppliers in the past when the world adopted a rule that restricted fishing boats from one nation from fishing within 200 mile of the coast of another country. Jumbo jets brought New England bluefin into easy reach of Japan and U.S. fishermen began to catch and export the large tuna. The 1980s were prosperous for Japan, which sustained the market for bluefin, but the economic bubble burst in the early 90s. Just in time, North Americans developed a taste for shushi, creating a strong market for the fish. As shushi became more and more popular in the United States, and later Europe, the expanded market increased fishing activity all across the Atlantic, and gave rise to fish farming, especially in Spanish and Croatian waters. But markets rely on supply and demand; in 1999 the Japanese managed to catch a year's supply of tuna in three days, reducing demand and prices. Prices also fell when environmental conditions in the Mediterranean resulted in reduced oxygen in the water. 800 tuna in a Spanish fish trap suffocated and were immediately caught and processed causing an oversupply that lowered tuna prices across the world.

Today, the market for tuna continues to thrive. The best bluefin still go to Japan where the market is still strongest, but the rest satisfy palates in many other parts of the world. Fishermen now often come in conflict with customers, governments, regulators and environmentalists around the world as they catch or farm tuna. Since tuna fishing is a local industry, local economies based on fishing may be instantly affected by changes in world prices for the fish.

Bestor also points out that a global market does not necessarily mean cultural homogenization. Sushi, he argues, is considered a Japanese delicacy no matter where in the world it is eaten. The article also includes two boxed inserts, one on the international regulations on fishing and the other on the workings of the Tsukiui fish market.

True or False?

F   1.   Bestor (How Sushi Went Global) notes that the Japanese love of sushi increased because the introduction of jet aircraft in the 1960s made it possible to ship fresh bluefin tuna, the centerpiece of sushi, to Japan before the fish could spoil.

T   2.   According to Bestor (How Sushi Went Global), few North Americans ate bluefin tuna before the international market for sushi developed, preferring, instead, to fish for tuna as a sport.

F   3.   Bestor (How Sushi Went Global) argues that the Japanese control the world price for bluefin tuna because the government sets prices paid for imported fish, which, in turn, affects the economy of U.S. fishing villages.

T   4.   According to Bestor (How Sushi Went Global), bluefin tuna are now raised in Spanish waters near Gibraltar where they are fed by hand.

F   5.   According to Bestor (How Sushi Went Global), America has become the sushi center of the world market for bluefin tuna and Japan has come to be on the periphery.

T   6.   Bestor (how Sushi Went Global) notes that Japan is still the central market for internationally caught bluefin tuna and the Japanese have tried to teach American fishermen and tuna buyers how to judge the quality of tuna that are suitable for the Japanese market.

Multiple Choice

1.   According to Bestor (How Sushi Went Global),
    a.   globalization does not mean homogenization. Sushi is still viewed as Japanese worldwide.
    b.   in Spanish waters off Gibraltar, bluefin tuna are trapped, fed by hand, then processed to meet the demand for sushi in Japan and around the world.
    c.   there is a national tuna day in Japan.
    d.   two of the above.
 * e   a, b, and c above.

2.   According to Bestor, the reason that Japanese had to turn to the world market for bluefin tuna was
    a.   they had completely fished out bluefin tuna in the Pacific.
 * b.   a world agreement prevented fishing within 200 miles of other countries' shores.
    c.   the Japanese discovered that Atlantic tuna were much better than their own Pacific tuna.
    d.   sushi became more popular in Japan in the 1960s so that demand outran supply.
    e.   the cost of bluefin tuna sold on the world market was much lower than the cost in Japanese markets.

3. According to Bestor (How Sushi Went Global), the world demand for sushi and its centerpiece, bluefin tuna, has resulted in four of the five outcomes listed below. Which one is **not** an outcome of this demand?
   a. Over fishing is threatening to reduce the number of bluefin tuna in the Atlantic
   b. The demand and increase in fishing to meet it have caused 28 countries to form a regulatory group called the "International Commission for the Conservation of Atlantic Tunas (ICCAT).
   c. There is a battle between U.S. regulators and fisherman and their European counterparts over unequal limits on the number of tuna that can be fished.
   * d. The U.S. has made a unilateral declaration that tuna fishing by foreign factory ships will not be permitted within 300 miles of its shores.
   e. The introduction of the *almadraba* system of fishing in the Spanish waters near Gilbratar.

4. Why does Bestor (How Sushi Went Global) refer to bluefin tuna as "stateless fish?"
   * a. Bluefin tuna swim so fast and migrate so far they may not remain in any nation's waters for long.
   b. ICCAT (the International Commission for the Conservation of Tunas), made up of 28 countries, has declared that the fish should receive "stateless" legal status.
   c. No one country has been willing to take responsibility for conserving bluefin tuna.
   d. Scientists have not been able to determine what state of mind the tuna are in.
   e. Blufin tuna form part of sushi in every country of the world.

5. According to Bestor (How Sushi Went Global), the Japanese control of sushi as a Japanese cultural entity is enhanced by all but one of the following. Which one is not something that has enhanced Japanese control?
   a. the migration of Japanese sushi chefs to other countries, so that sushi is often prepared by Japanese experts.
   b. the appearance of Japanese-named sushi bars in many countries
   * c. the licensing of bars and restaurants outside of Japan by the Japanese Bureau of Cultural Exportation (BCE)
   d. the use of Japanese décor and even Japanese language in restaurants and bars that serve sushi.
   e. all of the above

6. According to Bestor (How Sushi Went Global), Tsukiji, Tokyo's wholesale seafood market
   a. sets the world price for bluefin tuna.
   b. controls the supply of bluefin tuna by delaying their sale, sometimes for days.
   c. is sent daily information about tuna conditions in such fishing grounds as Monhtauk, Cape Cod, Cartagena by fisherman in return for information about prices.
   * d. two of the above.
   e. a, b, and c above.

PART 5

KINSHIP AND FAMILY

The introduction to Part 5 reviews a variety of basic concepts anthropologists use to describe kinship systems.

KEY DEFINITIONS

Kinship is the complex system of culturally defined social relationships based on marriage, the principle of affinity, and birth, the principle of consanguinity.

Affinity refers to relationships through marriage.

Consanguinity refers to relationships by blood.

Descent is a kinship rule that ties people together on the basis of reputed common ancestry.

Patrilineal descent is a descent rule linking consanguine relatives together through males only.

Matrilineal descent is a descent rule linking relatives together through females only.

Bilateral descent is a descent rule linking relatives together through both males and females simultaneously.

Descent groups are groups based on a descent rule.

A **lineage** is a localized group that is based on unilineal (patrilineal or matrilineal) descent and which usually has some corporate powers.

A **clan** is a descent group based on a unilineal rule of descent that is composed of lineages and whose members cannot always trace their genealogical relationship to all others.

Phratries are large unilineal kin groups made up of clans.

Ramages are cognatic kin groups based on bilateral descent, which resemble lineages in size and function but provide more recruiting flexibility.

A **family** is a kin group made up of at least one married couple sharing the same residence with their children and performing sexual, reproductive, economic, and educational functions.

A **nuclear family** is a kind of family consisting of just one married couple and their children.

An **extended family** is a family made up of two or more married couples and their children.

Marriage is the socially approved union of a man and a woman that confers sexual rights and legitimizes children.

Exogamy means marriage outside a specified group.

Endogamy means marriage inside a specified group.

Monogamy is a kind of marriage in which one man is married to one woman.

Polygamy is a kind of marriage in which one person is married to more than one person simultaneously.

Polygyny is a kind of marriage in which one man is married to two or more women simultaneously.

Polyandry is a kind of marriage in which one woman is married to two or more men simultaneously.

The **incest taboo** is a legal rule that prohibits sexual intercourse or marriage between particular classes of kin.

QUESTIONS

True or False?

T   1.   The marriage of one man to two or more women is called polygyny.

F   2.   If the people of a village prefer that their children marry spouses from other villages, they follow the rule of village endogamy.

T   3.   Descent is a rule of relationship that links people together on the basis of reputed common ancestry. It often serves to regulate inheritance and the formation of kin groups.

F   4.   A kinship group based on a unilineal rule of descent that is localized and which has corporate power is called a clan.

T 5. A family is a kin group made up of at least one married couple and their children, and which is residential and which has sexual, reproductive, economic, and educational functions.

Multiple Choice

1. _____ are unilineal descent groups composed of lineages. Their members recognize descent from a common ancestor, but cannot usually trace their actual genealogical connections.
    a. Ramages
    b. Kindreds
    * c. Clans
    d. Phratries
    e. Families

2. An older married couple, together with their married sons, their daughters-in-law, and their grandchildren, all living in a single household, is a classic example of
    a. a nuclear family.
    * b. an extended family.
    c. a lineage.
    d. a clan.
    e. a ramage.

3. Descent from a common ancestor through males only, is called
    * a. patrilineal descent.
    b. matrilineal descent.
    c. bilateral descent.
    d. exogamy.
    e. endogamy.

4. A bilateral kinship group that is most like the lineage is called
    a. family.
    b. clan.
    c. phratry.
    d. dormitory floor.
    * e. ramage.

5. A rule of relationship that links people together on the basis of reputed common ancestry is called
    a. affinity.
    * b. descent.
    c. patrilineality.
    d. marriage.
    e. social organization.

6. A person one is related to by marriage is called a(n) _____ relative.
 * a. affinal
   b. exogamous
   c. consanguine
   d. endogamous
   e. polygamous

7. The cultural rule that prohibits sexual intercourse among defined classes of relatives is called
 * a. the incest taboo.
   b. polygamy.
   c. endogamy.
   d. polygyny.
   e. hypergamy.

8. The marriage of one woman to more than one man simultaneously is called
   a. exogamy.
   b. endogamy.
   c. polygyny.
 * d. polyandry.
   e. polyglycol.

9. A relationship between a man and a woman that is socially recognized and which confers birth-status rights on children is called
   a. kinship.
   b. consanguineal.
   c. a family.
 * d. marriage.
   e. a rite of passage.

10. When a man is simultaneously married to two or more women, anthropologists call the arrangement
   a. polygamy.
 * b. polygyny.
   c. polyandry.
   d. the sororate.
   e. erogamy.

11. When it is preferred that a woman marry a man from her own village, we call the arrangement
   a. polygyny.
   b. exogamy.
 * c. endogamy.
   d. polyandry.
   e. levirate.

Article 20

Mother's Love: Death without Weeping **NANCY SCHEPER-HUGHES**

Summary In this article, Nancy Scheper-Hughes argues that under conditions of extreme poverty where there are high rates of infant mortality, it is a natural human response for mothers to distance themselves emotionally from their dead and dying children.

She bases her conclusion on 25 years of fieldwork experience in the shanty town of Alto do Cruzeiro on the edge of Bom Jesus de Mata, a market town in Northeast Brazil. Poverty in the shanty town produces a life expectancy of only 40 years, largely due to high rates of infant mortality. Social conditions are marked by brittle marriages; single parenting by women is the norm. Most work in the "shadow economy." Houses are most often built of daub and wattle and babies are frequently left home alone in them because infants can't be taken to work.

Scheper-Hughes first encountered women's reactions to infant death in 1965 when 350 children died in a "great baby die off." Mothers seemed strangely indifferent to the deaths of their children. It was then that Scheper-Hughes concluded that learning to mother in Alto do Cruzeiro meant learning to know when to let go of one's emotional ties to children who were sick or weak.

Subsequent fieldwork revealed that mothers are supported in their detachment by midwives and other women. Even civil authorities and the clergy try to discourage over attachment to babies. Registration of infant death is short and informal. Doctors don't recognize malnutrition and may just tranquilize, not treat, a dying child despite the fact that treatment might save the infant's life. The church no longer holds ceremonies for dead children, and infants are buried without headstones in spots that will be used over and over again.

Scheper-Hughes concludes that the lack of emotion over the death of their children is natural for women under these conditions, and that this reaction is seen in many parts of the world where infant death is common.

QUESTIONS

True or False?

T   1.   In her article, "Mother's Love: Death Without Weeping," Scheper-Hughes argues that mothers in the shanty town of Alto do Cruzeiro learn to accept the death of a child without grieving.

F   2.   According to Scheper-Hughes (Mother's Love: Death Without Weeping), poor women in northeast Brazil will sacrifice in every way possible to keep their children alive.

T 3. According to Scheper-Hughes, civil and church authorities in the northeast town of Bom Jesus de Mata, Brazil, treat infant death casually and without much concern.

F 4. According to Scheper-Hughes, the doctors and clergy of the Brazilian city of Bom Jesus de Mata work hard to save the lives of poor children born in the shanty town of Alto do Cruzeiro, but fail because of the indifference of the infants' mothers.

F 5. Nancy Scheper-Hughes (Mother's Love: Death without Weeping), feels that it is instinctual for poor mothers to grieve deeply over the death of their babies in most societies unless they have been separated from their infants by illness or divorce.

T 6. According to Scheper-Hughes (Mother's Love: Death without Weeping), mothers living in Alto do Cruzeiro in northeastern Brazil have been known to actually hasten the death of babies they feel will not survive by failing to feed them properly.

Multiple Choice

1. According to Scheper-Hughes in her article, "Mother's Love: Death without Weeping," poor Brazilian mothers living in a shanty town near the town of Bom Jesus de Mata
   a. will do almost anything to earn money in order to pay for the treatment of their sick babies.
   * b. stay emotionally detached from their babies, particularly those they feel are likely to die.
   c. depend for child support on the local churches and civil authorities.
   d. observe nearly a year of formal mourning when a child dies, during which time they are not allowed to dance or laugh in public.
   e. try not to have children since infants die so easily.

2. According to Scheper-Hughes, doctors in the Brazilian town of Bom Jesus de Mata often
   * a. fail to recognize malnutrition as the primary cause of illness among poor babies.
   b. refuse to examine poor babies.
   c. prescribe drugs that their mothers can not afford to buy for their sick babies.
   d. hospitalize poor sick babies because the infants' mothers can't care for them.
   e. claim poor mothers are killing their babies through neglect.

3. Scheper-Hughes reports that about _____ infants died in Alto do Cruzeiro, Brazil, in 1965.
   a. 100
   b. 150
   c. 250
   d. 300
   * e. 350

4. According to Scheper-Hughes, four of the following statements are true about how the death of poor babies is treated in Alto do Cruzeiro and Bom Jesus de Mata, Brazil. Which one is **not**?
   a. babies are buried without headstones or markers
   b. the church rarely holds ceremonies for dead infants
   c. the grave where an infant is buried may be used again for another later
   * d. midwives encourage mothers of dead babies to grieve
   e. civil authorities only require a two-paragraph report when a baby dies

5. On the basis of her work in northeastern Brazil and on literature describing practices in other parts of the world, Scheper-Hughes feels that
   a. it is instinctual for mothers to grieve deeply over a dead son or daughter in every society including those with high infant mortality rates.
   b. poor mothers everywhere cannot help but become attached to their sickly infants even though the latter are likely to die.
   * c. it is natural for poor mothers to maintain emotional distance from infants who are likely to die.
   d. civil authorities try hard to improve the condition of poor women but the latter won't help themselves.
   e. poor women let their babies die despite concerted efforts by church authorities to prevent them from doing so.

6. Scheper-Hughes (Mother's Love: Death Without Weeping) claims that which of the follow kinds of people encourages mothers not to become attached to their sick and dying children?
   a. clergy
   b. doctors
   c. midwives
   d. two of the above
   * e. a, b, and c above

Article 21

Family and Kinship in Village India

DAVID W. McCURDY

Summary In this article, David McCurdy describes the importance of kinship among rural Bhil tribal peoples living in Ratakote, a hill village located in the southern part of Rajasthan near Udaipur, India. He argues that an elaborate and extended kinship system is not only a useful way for peasants to organize their labor, land holdings, and broader social connections, but that it is also a system that can be adapted to the market-dominated economic system currently emerging in India.

Americans find it difficult to comprehend the importance of extended kinship, but for the Bhils, the significance of kinship seems elementary. A wedding arranged by a villager for his daughter in 1985 illustrates the point nicely. To begin the arrangement, the father must consult the members of his patrilineage, who must later provide money and labor for the wedding. He will send out word to his feminal kin, the relatives of the women who have married into his line and the relatives of the men that women of his line have married in other villages. When prospective grooms are found, the first consideration is clan membership. Clans are large and consist of local lineages living in many villages over a wide territory. Bhils cannot marry into their own, their mother's, or their father's mother's clans without committing incest.

Once a suitable spouse is found, negotiations commence to set a bride price, the money and prestige goods given by the groom's family to that of the bride. Bride price is part of an exchange for the labor and loyalty of the bride. Marriage becomes an alliance between the two families but involves potential conflict. To clearly state that rights to her loyalty, labor, and children shifts to her husband's family at marriage, the wedding ceremony symbolizes the bride's removal from her natal group. After marriage, a relationship built on formal respect keeps the bride's family at a proper distance.

Extended kinship systems seem well suited to agrarian peasant life where landholding and economic production are best controlled by families. Today, India is industrializing and the market economy is attracting many rural peasants to cities as well as restructuring economic relationships in rural villages. The market economy can easily weaken kinship systems by providing individuals with salaries and independence, causing people to move to find work, and creating jobs that compete for time with family obligations. Despite expansion of the market, Indians, including the Bhils described in this article, have adapted kinship relationships to provide support as they scatter across their country and around the world.

QUESTIONS

True or False?

T 1. In his article, "Family and Kinship in Village India," McCurdy argues that family and kinship relations have been extended to provide support in the market economy.

F 2. According to McCurdy, until recently Bhil tribals were permitted to marry people from their own village, thus limiting the scope of their economic and social worlds.

F 3. According to McCurdy (Family and Kinship in Village India), marriage allies the families of the bride and groom, which then become equal partners in an association of feminal kin.

T 4. According to McCurdy, the term *feminal kin* refers to the relatives of the men who women of one's own line have married, or the relatives of women who have married men of one's own line.

T. 5. McCurdy notes that when a groom ritually breaks into his future bride's front yard at the beginning of the final wedding ceremony, the act is one way to symbolize her movement from her natal family to his.

F 6. McCurdy notes that clans are localized organizations of relatives made up of a person's close male relatives who are all descended from a known common ancestor.

Multiple Choice

1. According to McCurdy (Family and Kinship in Village India),
   * a. extended kinship systems are especially well suited to the organization of land holding in agrarian societies.
   b. industrialization and the market economy have essentially eliminated extended kinship ties in the Bhil village of Ratakote.
   c. the Bhil tribals of Ratakote must marry spouses from their own clan, their mother's clan, or their father's mother's clan.
   d. two of the above.
   e. none of the above.

2. According to McCurdy (Family and Kinship in Village India), the term *feminal kin* refers to _____ when it is used to described kin relationships in Ratakote.
   a. the women belonging to one's own patriclan (*arak*)
   b. the women belonging to one's mother's patriclan (*arak*)
   * c. the husbands and their relatives of women who belong to one's own lineage
   d. the women who make up one's matriclan
   e. men who take on the role of women

3. McCurdy (Family and Kinship in Village India) argues that arranged marriage functions to
   a. cement relationships within Bhil families and patrilineages.
   * b. create alliances between Bhil families and patrilineages.
   c. bring wealth to the groom's family because of the dowry they receive.
   d. prevent the possibility of divorce in Bhil society.
   e. insure a happier marriage for Bhil brides and grooms.

4. According to McCurdy, which one of the following is the most important structural tension associated with marriage in Bhil Society?
   a. the decision about how large the *dapa* (bride price) will be
   b. the possibility that young people will refuse to be married
   c. disagreement between lineages over who will get to give the wedding and receive the bride price
   * d. the shifting of a woman's loyalty, labor, and reproductive potential from her family to her husband's family.
   e. whether or not wives will inherit from their own or their husband's families

5. According to McCurdy, when Bhils visit other villages, they usually stay with
   a. members of their patrilineage.
   b. members of their patriclan.
   c. friends, not kin.
   d. members of their extended family.
   * e. feminal kin.

6. According to McCurdy, a major tension in Bhil society occurs over the movement of a woman from her own family to that of her husband at marriage. Which of the following is a way Bhil cultural practice functions to reduce this tension?
   a. grooms ritually storm the bride's front yard to symbolize that they are taking the woman away from her family
   b. after the wedding, the family of the bride treats the groom and his family with formal respect behavior
   c. the groom's family pays the family of the bride *dapa* (bride price) to compensate them for the loss of their daughter
   d. two of the above
   * e. a, b, and c above

7. According to McCurdy, work in the market economy can weaken kinship systems by
   a. costing families too much money.
   b. reducing the economic dependence of people on their families and kin groups.
   c. reducing the time people have to devote to family and kin.
   * d. two of the above.
   e. a, b, and c above.

8. McCurdy (Family and Kinship in Village India) observes that
    * a. despite the dispersal of relatives as a result of migration to cities for work, Indians maintain a high degree of loyalty to and support of their kin.
    b. work in cities has dramatically weakened the Indian family and kinship system.
    c. cash labor has led to personal independence and the end of family arranged marriages in India.
    d. two of the above.
    e. none of the above.

Article 22

Matrilineal Kinship:
Walking Marriage in China

LU YUAN AND SAM MITCHELL

Summary The Nari, called Mosuo by outsiders (and the name used in the article), are located in southwestern China along the shores of Lugu Lake on the border between Yunnan and Sichuan Provinces. They are a matrilineal group among whom women head most households and control most family property. The group is probably related to Tibetans although they consider themselves descended from Mongols because some of the latter settled and farmed where they live. They make their living by farming and fishing. Notably, marriage, in the sense of a formal socially recognized union between a man and a woman, among the Mosuo is uncommon. Instead, women take lovers who come to visit them but who return to their mother's house. Children stay with their mothers, and brothers look after their sisters. The Masuo call this arrangement with lovers, "walking marriage," but there is no formal union, making this the only society known where marriage is absent. (The Nayar of South India had an arrangement that resembled the Mosuo system but included a wedding ceremony to announce a young woman's eligibility for suitors. The ceremony did not lead to a permanent union, however.) The Masuo arrangement produces an unusual extended family, one made up of women, their children, and other males of the line. In essence, a woman's brothers fulfill many of the non-sexual functions normally associated with the role of husbands. A man's sister's children will care for him when he gets old. Masuo claim that this living arrangement prevents conflict because lovers rarely see each other and people are used the relationship.

The Masuo came in conflict with the Chinese government during the cultural revolution of 1966-1976. Classed even today as "living fossils," they were forced to marry in "proper" Chinese fashion during the revolution. During this period, men lived in their wives' houses but still worked at their maternal homes. They resumed "walking marriage" after the revolution. Lake Lugo is now open to tourists and many Masuo are learning Chinese and wearing Han cloths. The authors report that a Masuo leader feels that these changes may eventually alter his people's way of life and that the traditional Han patrilineal marriage system may eventually replace walking marriage.

QUESTIONS

True or False?

T 1. According to Yuan and Mitchell (Walking Marriage in China), women take lovers, not husbands, and form families with their brothers and children.

F 2. Yuan and Mitchell (Walking Marriage in China) note that Masuo women prefer to marry men from important families who live in other communities.

T   3.   According to Yuan and Mitchell (Walking Marriage in China}, the Masuo represent the only society where marriage is absent.

F   4.   Yuan and Mitchell (Walking Marriage in China), note that the Masuo living on Lugu Lake are a patrilineal group in which women take lovers rather than marry husbands.

F   5.   Yuan and Mitchell (Walking Marriage in China) show that the matrilineal Masuo of China became patrilineal and adopted formal marriage permanently after the cultural revolution of the 1960s and 70s.

F   6.   Yuan and Mitchell (Walking Masrriage in China) report that a Masuo leader feels that the traditional system where women take lovers rather than husbands in marriage will disappear because there is so much conflict between a woman's lovers.

Multiple Choice

1.   According to Yuan and Mitchell (Walking Marriage in China), Masuo women
     a.   are betrothed at birth and married by the time they are 14 years old.
   * b.   never married and take lovers during the years when they are sexually mature.
     c.   take lovers and live without the support of men in women-headed families.
     d.   live in patrilineal extended families.
     e.   preserve the patriline by marrying their cross-cousins.

2.   According to Yuan and Mitchell (Walking Marriage in China), the Masuo conform to the descent rule called
   * a.   matrilineality
     b.   patrilineality
     c.   bilaterality
     d.   avunculineality
     e.   matri-patrilineality

3.   According to Yuan and Mitchell (Walking Marriage in China), the Masuo live in families made up of
     a.   a woman, her husband, and her children.
     b.   a woman, her brothers, and her brothers' children.
   * c.   a woman, her brothers, her children, and other members of the matriline.
     d.   a woman and her children.
     e.   both her own and her husband's line members.

4. According to Yuan and Mitchell (Walking Marriage in China), the _____ of South India are the only society where marriage is largely absent and women take lovers.
    a. Bhils
    b. Badaga
    c. Nuer
*   d. Nayar
    e. Brahmins

5. According to Yuan and Mitchell, members of the Chinese government, using the classifications of an early American anthropologist, Lewis Henry Morgan, classified the Masuo sexual arrangement between Masuo men and women as
*   a. group marriage
    b. promiscuity
    c. polygyny
    d. polyandry
    e. polygamy

Article 23

Uterine Families and the Women's Community   MARGERY WOLF

Summary Anthropologists have traditionally looked at patrilineal society from the male point of view. In this article based largely on fieldwork on Taiwan in the late 50s and early 60s, Margery Wolf deals with the place of Chinese women in a patrilineal descent system. She focuses especially on how women establish their identity and security inside this apparently male world. A Chinese woman never holds a secure place in the patrilineal family of her birth. She will leave it at marriage and will not produce its heirs. When she enters her husband's family, she often meets with hostility and suspicion. The males view the bride as a producer of new members for the family, but the other women fear displacement at the hands of the new arrival. Therefore, a woman has to establish herself in her husband's family by building her own unit of support. Called the uterine family, the unit is composed of her offspring, particularly her sons who will remain with the family. Supported by her uterine family, a woman gains importance within her husband's extended family.

As she grows up, a girl uses her mother's uterine family as her model. After marriage, she may lose touch with her sisters, but she will always maintain strong ties with her brothers, who will have an important relationship with her children. In addition to the family network, she will also establish herself in the woman's community of her husband's village, and collectively she and the other women will exert influence over the behavior of other men and women.

QUESTIONS

True or False?

T   1.   A uterine family is composed of a woman and her children.

F   2.   Even after her marriage, a woman maintains close ties with her parents and siblings, according to Wolf in her article about the Chinese family.

F   3.   In a Chinese family, women are at the mercy of their husband's family throughout life, without recourse to the support of other people.

T   4.   The fact that Chinese women find support in their uterine families is a reason for conflict within their husband's extended family.

F   5.   A Chinese woman enters her husband's house as a powerless stranger, but she returns to her own home for visits during the first two or three years to reduce the tension.

T   6.   Much of the hostility between a woman and her mother-in-law comes about because of the ambiguous position of her husband.

Multiple Choice

1.   In her article on the Chinese uterine family, Wolf asserts that, within her husband's family
    a.   a Chinese woman depends almost solely on her husband for support.
    b.   a woman receives most support from her husband's brother's wives.
* c.   a woman receives most of her support from her children.
    d.   a woman receives most support from the families into which her daughters have married.
    e.   a woman receives most support from her parents and siblings.

2.   As a child, a Chinese woman's most important family ties are with her
    a.   father.
    b.   father's brothers.
    c.   father's mother.
* d.   mother and siblings.
    e.   siblings.

3.   The uterine family described by Wolf for China would include which one of the following after she is married
* a.   a woman's children.
    b.   a woman's brothers.
    c.   a woman's sisters.
    d.   a woman's sisters-in-law.
    e.   a woman's father.

4.   In her article, "Uterine Families and the Women's Community," Margery Wolf asserts that Taiwanese women
    a.   must always depend on their husbands for support in family affairs.
    b.   band together with the wives of their husband's brothers to achieve intrafamily power.
* c.   gain power by having sons.
    d.   gain power from the families their daughters marry into.
    e.   gain the most power by working hard at family tasks.

5.   According to Margery Wolf, which one of the following would be a member of her uterine family after she is married?
    a.   her mother-in-law
* b.   her sons
    c.   her brothers
    d.   her sisters
    e.   her mother

6. The Chinese depicted by Margery Wolf in the article about uterine families would best be classified as
    a. matrilineal.
    b. bilateral.
    c. clan endogamous.
    d. neolineal.
    * e. patrilineal.

PART 6

ROLES AND INEQUALITY

The introduction to Part 6 reviews basic elements of social organization and social inequality.

KEY DEFINITIONS

Social statuses are the categories of different kinds of people who interact.

Social roles are the rules for action associated with particular statuses.

Social situations are the settings in which interaction takes place. They include places, times, objects, and events.

Social Stratification is a form of inequality characterized by regularly experienced unequal access to valued economic resources and prestige.

Class is a kind of social stratification that restricts individuals' access to valued resources and prestige within a partially flexible system. Social mobility between classes is possible although often difficult.

Caste defines a second kind of social stratification, one based on permanent membership by birth without the possibility of social mobility between castes.

An **egalitarian society** is a kind of society that lacks formal social stratification, although inequality based on age and gender is possible.

A **rank** society is one in which there is unequal access to prestige, but not to valued economic resources.

A **stratified society** is marked by unequal access to both prestige and valued economic resources.

QUESTIONS

True or False?

T   1.   The rules for action associated with statuses are called "roles."

F 2. Roles are the categories of different kinds of people who interact.

F 3. An army private must salute when he approaches an officer and hold the salute until after the officer has returned the greeting. This is a description of a status.

F 4. As used in this book, the term status refers to a person's social rank.

T 5. A lecture, classroom, desks, and time (9:30-10:20) are all parts of the social situation as that term is defined by the text.

F 6. Anthropologists usually recognize two kinds of social stratification: egalitarian and rank.

T 7. Class is a kind of stratification defined by unequal access to prestige and valued resources but which permits individual mobility.

F 8. A "rank society" is one in which members have unequal access to prestige and valued economic resources.

Multiple Choice

1. The culturally defined positions associated with particular social structures are labeled
    a. roles.
    * b. statuses.
    c. social situations.
    d. social groups.
    e. events.

2. Social situations consist of a combination of culturally appropriate
    a. times.
    b. places.
    c. objects.
    d. two of the above.
    * e. a, b, and c above.

3. If a friend were to say, "He's the president of the college," the term "president" would refer to a(n)
    * a. status.
    b. role.
    c. social situation.
    d. social relationship.
    e. social interaction.

4. Class is to caste as
    a. western is to non western.
    b. equality is to rank.
    c. economics is to prestige.
    d. equality is to social stratification.
  * e. open is to closed.

5. A society in which there is unequal access to prestige but equal access to economic resources is called a(n)
    a. egalitarian society.
    b. socially stratified society.
  * c. rank society.
    d. caste society.
    e. class society.

6. The culturally defined behaviors associated with particular social statuses are called
    a. social identities.
  * b. social roles.
    c. status clusters.
    d. social action clusters.
    e. social actionality .

7. A group ranked in a system of social stratification into which members are born for life is called a
  * a. caste.
    b. class.
    c. rank society.
    d. stratified society.
    e. bounded society.

8. Lecture, desks, class hours and writing boards are all part of the class
    a. stratification.
    b. rank.
  * c. social situation.
    d. status.
    e. role.

Article 24

Symbolizing Roles: Behind the Veil

**ELIZABETH W. FERNEA AND
ROBERT A. FERNEA**

Summary In this article, Elizabeth and Robert Fernea discuss a key symbol in Middle Eastern society, the veil worn by women, which often completely covers the head, face, and body. For many Westerners, the Middle Eastern veil stands for the subjugation of women, although some find it sexually titillating. For Middle Easterners, the veil has many important meanings. Above all the veil stands for *purdah*, the seclusion of women. It signals the public power of men and the unavailability of women to other men. It stands for women's most important value, her honor, and it indicates wealth, for only wealthy people can afford female seclusion. It is also associated with the city, where women should be protected against the gaze of strangers. And it stands for a woman's private space and personal protection, giving her a comfortable anonymity in public. In short, it symbolizes a set of values and conditions in a society where men and women are viewed as different and where there is a strong value on female chastity and honor.

QUESTIONS

True or False?

F   1.   Elizabeth and Robert Fernea feel that the veil is disappearing in Middle Eastern society because of a changing value on the respective roles of men and women.

T   2.   According to the Ferneas, the Middle Eastern veil is closely related to the custom of *purdah*.

F   3.   Middle Eastern women find the veil hot and uncomfortable but wear it because their husbands require them to.

F   4.   According to the Ferneas, veiling is most often found in rural parts of the Middle East.

T   5.   According to the Ferneas, one of the meanings of the veil is a welcome anonymity for females in public places.

T   6.   The veil, according to the Ferneas, means the protection of family honor and is related to a belief that women are unable to control their sexuality.

Multiple Choice

1. According to Elizabeth and Robert Fernea, the Middle Eastern veil stands for _____ for most people from Western countries.
    a.   female honor
    * b.   female slavery
    c.   gender equality
    d.   wealth
    e.   protection

2. In their article on the veil, the Ferneas' main purpose is to
    a.   trace the history of the veil in the Middle East from earliest times to the present.
    b.   show how the veil is used by males to subjugate females.
    * c.   describe the meaning of the veil.
    d.   show how the veil is used by women to protect themselves.
    e.   reveal the symbolic importance of the veil in modern conservative Middle Eastern religious movements.

3. According to the Ferneas, the honor (*ard*) of a woman depends on only one thing,
    a.   loyalty to the family.
    b.   how she is dressed.
    c.   hard work.
    * d.   chastity.
    e.   all of the above.

4. Unlike Western feminists, most Middle Eastern women continue to believe that
    * a.   men and women are biologically different.
    b.   men and women are biologically the same.
    c.   men are superior to women.
    d.   women are superior to men.
    e.   women should not defer to their husband's wishes.

5. According to the Ferneas, the term *purdah* means
    a.   the veil worn by women in India.
    b.   female honor in the Middle East.
    c.   the value on male superiority.
    * d.   the seclusion of women.
    e.   the part of the veil covering a woman's face.

6. The Ferneas argue that the Middle Eastern veil symbolizes
    * a.   female honor, wealth, and urban life.
      b.   protection, female slavery, and wealth.
      c.   health, female slavery, and honor.
      d.   modernization and equality.
      e.   feminism and female power.

Article 25

Society and Sex Roles   ERNESTINE FRIEDL

Summary In recent years, many anthropologists have argued that males inherit the predisposition to dominate females. In this article, Friedl argues against this position. Instead, she asserts, control of resources that are shared publicly (beyond the family) is the key to power and dominance. In support of her position, she looks at four kinds of hunting and gathering societies. The first, characterized by cooperative male and female labor in foraging, demonstrates sexual equality. The Washo are an example of such a society. The second type also displays equality, largely because men and women forage separately and work to meet their own individual needs. The third type, illustrated by the Tiwi, manifests inequality. Men hunt and control the public distribution of meat; women gather only for family needs. Finally, the fourth type, represented by the Eskimo, is characterized by the provision of food, in this case meat, by men. In such societies women are "used, abused, and traded." In many agriculturally based societies, men control most of the food that is exchanged, and women's status remains correspondingly low. But in industrial societies, women have begun to limit the number of children they have and in some cases gain control of goods for distribution beyond the family. If this pattern continues, Friedl concludes, we could have a society that approaches the sexual equality displayed by the Washo.

QUESTIONS

True or False?

F   1.   Friedl believes that women have gained greater equality with men as societies have evolved toward more complex forms.

T   2.   Friedl believes that control of resources that are publicly allocated is the key to equality and inequality between the sexes.

T   3.   According to Friedl, the Washo Indians displayed sexual equality because men and women worked together to produce food.

F   4.   Friedl believes that when women control public resources, they come to dominate men.

T   5.   Friedl reports that the Semai of Malaya are afraid of violence, so that a man would never strike a woman there.

T   6.   Friedl feels that men dominate women in most of the world's societies.

Multiple Choice

1. In her article on sex roles, Friedl argues that the key to women's power is
    a. control over family finances.
    b. having a large number of children.
    c. their contribution of goods and services toward family maintenance.
    * d. control of goods and services distributed out side the family.
    e. wider societal values on equality.

2. Ernestine Friedl claims that, based on evidence from hunter/gatherer societies as well as other cases, women
    a. can attain equal power with men.
    b. can come to exercise power over men.
    c. inherit the tendency to be subordinate.
    d. cannot usually attain the same power as men in industrial society.
    * e. can attain equal status with men.

3. According to Friedl, women have the least power in relation to men in which one of the following societies?
    a. Washo
    * b. Eskimo
    c. Tiwi
    d. !Kung
    e. Tiv

4. The key to male power in hunting and gathering society is their
    a. control over the movement of the band.
    b. superior physical strength.
    * c. control over the supply of animal protein.
    d. control over the political process.
    e. trading connections to other bands.

5. As part of her argument about the relative power of men and women in hunter/gatherer societies, Friedl argues that men universally
    a. wield more power than women.
    b. determine the movements of the band.
    c. distribute food to family members.
    * d. do all the big game hunting.
    e. do all the collecting of plants.

6. According to Friedl, the amount of power wielded by men in hunter/gatherer society is directly related to
   a. the volume of vegetable matter they can collect.
   b. the volume of vegetable matter women can collect.
   c. whether or not women hunt big game.
   d. their control over the political process.
 * e. the availability and abundance of big game in the environment.

Article 26

Mixed Blood

JEFFREY M. FISH

Summary This article argues that the American concept of race is culturally constructed, not a biological reality. The issue is important since psychologists and other scientists often treat races as if they were biological realities.

Human beings form a single species but display physical variations that have occurred through the processes of random mutation, natural selection, and genetic drift (accidental selection). Americans believe that people can be classed into biological races on the basis of these variations. Races are typically defined in biology as localized breeding populations that display a set of physical traits that cluster together (covary). Fish argues that no modern human populations can be found that fit these criteria because no human groups display clusters of traits that co vary. [Ed. note: Some anthropologists believe that Neandertals were a race because they were found in one part of the world and share a cluster of distinctive physical traits not seen elsewhere.] The reason for this is that most traits that Americans think of as racial, such as skin color, are adaptive and vary with environmental conditions. Biological races, Fish concludes, do not exist.

If races are not biologically distinguishable groups, what are they? The answer is simple: they are arbitrary folk classifications of people based on culturally selected criteria. People everywhere classify things in folk taxonomies, but classifications of the same things may vary arbitrarily from society to society. Americans classify avocados as a vegetable and eat them in salads. Brazilians classify avocados as a fruit and eat them with lemon and sugar for desert. Americans classify people as black, white, Latino, and Asian. Brazilians classify them into *tipos* (types) including *loura* (completely blond), *branca* (light-skinned) *morena* (tan skin with black or brown hair), *mulata* (slightly darker with more curley hair), *preta* (dark skin, broader nose), sarará (tight curly blond or red hair, blue eyes, broad nose and think lips) and *cabo verde* (straight black hair, dark skin, brown eyes, narrow nose, and thin lips).

Brazilians classify people on the basis of what they look like. Americans classify them on the basis of how their parents are classified using the principle of *hypo-descent*. Americans rank races; white is highest, followed by Asian, Hispanic (Latino), and black. Children are given the racial classification of their lowest- (hypo) ranking parent. If your mother is classed as black and your father white, you will be classified as black no matter what you look like. A single Brazilian couple, on the other hand, may have their children classified into different *tipos* because each looks different from each others.

The meaning of race in America is especially important when scientists use these categories as if they were biological entities and attempt to correlate such things as IQ, behavior, and disease susceptibility with them. Since American races are not biologically determined, such correlations are spurious.

The American conception of race is beginning to change as more people of different "races" intermarry and immigrants whose racial identity is difficult to classify by the American system enter the country. "Other" is a growing category of racial identity.

Fish concludes that by taking a plane to Brazil, his daughter can change her race from black to *moreno* (Fish is by American standards white, his wife is a Brazilian anthropologist). Like avocados, their daughter's racial identity is subject to different cultural classifications in different societies.

QUESTIONS

True or False?

T 1. In his article, "Mixed Blood," Fish argues that the American concept of race is culturally constructed, not a biological reality

F 2. According to Fish, human beings cannot be classified into races on the basis of physical characteristics because there is so little variation within the human species.

T 3. According to Fish (Mixed Blood), avocados are classified by Brazilians as a fruit and by North Americans as a vegetable.

F 4. According to Fish, North Americans fail in their attempt to classify people into races because they ignore important physical differences such as body shape (rounded and lanky for example).

T 5. According to Fish, Brazilians classify people into *tipos* such as *loura*, *branca*, *morena*, *mulata*, and *preta* on the basis of how they look.

F 6. Fish argues that scientists, such as psychologists, use the concept of hypo-descent to choose the physical characteristics that determine biological races.

Multiple Choice

1. According to Fish, the American conception of race is
   a. based on what people look like.
 * b. based on the racial identity of one's parents.
   c. ignores the principle of hypo-descent.
   d. parallels the way Brazilians classify races.
   e. is based on biological reality.

2. According to Fish (Mixed Blood), human biological variety is caused by
   a. mutation.
   b. natural selection.
   c. genetic drift.
   d. only two of the above.
   * e. all of the above.

3. Fish (Mixed Blood) argues that human biological races do not exist because
   * a. human physical characteristics, such as skin color and nose shape, do not covary.
   b. scientists have ignored important physical traits such as body shape.
   c. people find it politically incorrect to name them.
   d. the real traits that indicate genetic groupings cannot be observed.
   e. none of the above.

4. According to Fish (Mixed Blood), his daughter can change her race by flying from New York to Brazil. She can do this because
   a. Brazilians don't know what her North American racial classification is.
   * b. Brazilians have a different set of racial categories than do North Americans.
   c. she can claim to be any race she wants because there are no such things as biological races.
   d. airplanes provide a computer program that permits people to change their racial designation.
   e. although she is classed as white in the U.S., she can become *loura, preta,* or *tipo* in Brazil.

5. According to Fish (Mixed Blood), the terms *moreno, loura, branca,* and *preta* all refer to
   a. particular physical characteristics Brazilians use to assign people to what they call *tipos.*
   b. areas of Brazil after which groups of people are named.
   * c. Brazilian names for different *tipos* (types).
   d. areas of Brazil from which particular *tipos* are thought to have originated.
   e. a folk taxonomy of skin colors starting with black and ending with white.

6. According to Fish (Mixed Blood), an avocado is classed as a _____ in the U.S. and a _____ in Brazil.
   a. fruit: seed
   b. seed: nut
   c. vegetable: nut
   * d. vegetable: fruit
   e. nut;   seed

7. Fish (Mixed Blood) refers to the list of Brazilian *tipos* as
   a. biological races.
   * b. a folk taxonomy.
   c. political biased.
   d. incorrect.
   e. castes.

Article 27

Blood on the Steppes:
Ethnicity, Power, and Conflict

JACK WEATHERFORD

Summary This article by Jack Weatherford looks at how different groups living in Central Asia have chosen and use ethnic identities. Many people think that ethnic identity is always a resurrection of past tribal or national membership. Weatherford argues that identities can be changed and shaped by current necessities and possibilities. He cites cases from Central Asia where a number of countries have recently become independent from Russia and have had to develop ethnic identities of their own.

Weatherford's first case, the Mongols, appear to follow what most would consider the normal path to ethnic identity. Mongolians have resurrected their ancient pre communist culture, especially the customs and symbols suppressed by the Russians. They have torn down the Soviet stars, hammers, and sickles and put up images of Genghis Khan. Gone are the farming collectives. In their place, Mongolians are returned to a life on the steppes, herding animals and living in *gers* (felt tents). The return to the past has not occurred out of nostalgia; it is an economic necessity. When the Russians departed, Mongolia was economically cut off from the rest of the world. The pastoral life style reemerged because it was economically adaptive for a people without exports and money to sustain the imported vehicles and cement buildings found in other countries.

Other newly independent republics of Central Asia with stronger economies have used different strategies to achieve national identities. In Uzbekistan, the government chose to create its identity around their Uzbec national hero, Tamerlane. The choice favored the Uzbek inhabitants and most of the Russians, Ukrainians, Tartars, and Germans who also lived there decided to leave. In Turkmenistan, the president of the country decided to emphasize the tribal identity of Turkomen. Lacking a Turkomen hero, he set himself up as the heroic symbol of the tribe.

Many groups have turned to religion as the basis of their identity. The Uighurs, a Turkic-speaking people of Xinjiang, a province in China, have adopted religion (Islam) to symbolize their ethnicity. Because they can't display religious symbols in China, they have chosen a secular heroine, Fragrant Concubine, to stand for their Muslim identity. Although Chinese authorities have attempted to eradicate the religion by executing Uighurs, their actions have only stepped up the Uighur movement toward Islamic fundamentalism.

Identity has even formed around criminal activity. A group of men who illegally fish in the Ili estuary where it joins lake Balkhash in Kazakhstan, have formed a group called the Reebok mafia. (The Russian word for fisherman is *rebak*.) Because it sounds similar to their occupation, they have adopted clothing and symbols of the Reebok sports company to proclaim their special identity. The group is made up of people who identified once as Russians, Mongols, Kirghiz, and Germans but have found a common identity associated with their occupation. Thus, ethnic identity can be put to many uses "from subsistence and politics to crime and religion."

QUESTIONS

True or False?

F   1.   In his article on ethnicity, power, and conflict, Weatherford argues that ethnic identity is by definition a resurrection of a group's historical ethnic identity.

T   2.   According to Weatherford (Blood on the Steppes), Mongolians have returned to their pre communist pastoral culture because it is the only way of life that is currently economically viable.

F   3.   According to Weatherford (Blood on the Steppes), Uzbeks have created a national identity around their culture hero, Genghis Khan.

T   4.   Weatherford notes that a group fishing illegally in the Ili estuary of Lake Balkash have decided to identify with the Reebok Company, wearing its clothing and symbols and calling themselves the Reebok Mafia.

T   5.   Weatherford notes that the Uighurs living in Xinjiang, a province in China, have adopted Islam as a way to identify themselves as a separate group and have made a secular heroine, Fragrant Concubine, into a religious saint because they aren't allowed standard religious symbols.

T   6.   According to Weatherford (Blood on the Steppes), the president of Turkmenostan has made himself the hero of the newly resurrected Turkomen tribal identity in that country.

Multiple Choice

1.   In his article, "Blood on the Steppes," Weatherford argues that many Central Asian peoples
   a.   have revolted against their former Soviet and Chinese masters.
   b.   have adopted democratic governments after long revolts.
   * c.   have developed new ethnic identities based on their old cultures and culture heros, or religion and even a sports company.
   d.   have replaced communist rule with socialist governments of their own.
   e.   have united to form a pan-Asian confederation.

2. Weatherford points out that the Mongols, now free of dependence on Russia, have used _____ to symbolize their new identity.
    a. Tamerlane
    b. Turkomen
    c. Fragrant Concubine
    * d. Genghis Khan
    e. the Reebok company

3. According to Weatherford (Blood on the Steppes), the Mongolians have
    a. turned to their old cultural identity based on pastoralism because of their reverence for Genghis Kahn.
    * b. resurrected their traditional pastoral culture because it is the only economically viable way to live on the steppes.
    c. turned to their old cultural identity based on pastoralism because of their reverence for Tamerlane.
    d. turned to Islam for their cultural identity.
    e. began to revere a secular heroine, Fragrant Concubine, because the Chinese would not let them have their traditional religious symbols.

4. According to Weatherford (Blood on the Steppes), a group of men who fish illegally in the Ili estuary of Lake Balkhash have adopted _____ as their source of group identity.
    * a. the Reebok company
    b. Islam
    c. Turkomen
    d. Genghis Kahn
    e. Tamerlane

5. According to Weatherford (Blood on the Steppes), Uighurs living in Xinjiang, a province in China, have adopted the secular figure _____ to symbolize their _____ identity.
    a. Tamerlane: Islamic
    b. Genghis Kahn: Turkic
    c. Reebok: fishing
    d. Turkomen: Turkic
    * e. Fragrant Concubine: Islamic

6. According to Weatherford (Blood on the Steppes), ethnic identity
    * a. is a cultural construction that can change over time.
    b. is based on biologically defined traits and is immutable.
    c. is a cultural construction of how a group used to be.
    d. is a historical fact that lasts through time.
    e. none of the above.

7. Weatherford (Blood on the Steppes) notes that ethnic identities of Central Asian peoples have recently been built around
    a. religion.
    b. heroic historical figures.
    c. economic necessity.
    d. tribal ancestry.
  * e. all of the above.

Article 28

New Americans: The Road to Refugee Resettlement   DIANNA SHANDY

Summary In this article, Dianna Shandy, who has conducted ethnographic research among Nuer refugees in the upper Midwest since 1997, looks at what their status as refugee means, how they managed to come to the United states, why they were located in more than 30 different U.S. states, how a people raised as cattle herders survive and adapt to life in a U.S. urban setting, and what this tells us about "the interconnectedness of a globalizing world and anthropology's role in it."

Although no special categories were assigned to people who first migrated to the U.S. (they were all simply called immigrants), today there are at least two, migrants and refugees, based on their reasons for coming here. The UN defines refugees as people who have left a country because of a well-founded fear of persecution based on race, religion, nationality; membership in a particular social group, or political opinion. They are not merely IDPs (internally displaced persons) who have left home but are willing to return. To manage the refugee "problem" (by 2000 there were 20 million refugees in the world), there is a UN Agency headed by a high commissioner for refugees (UNHCR). The UN and many countries see three solutions for refugee placement: voluntary repatriation, integration into a country of asylum, or rarely, third country resettlement. Typically, refugees are first housed in camps, and then certified for resettlement. The U.S. takes in a limited number of refugees and employs the UN criteria for refugee certification. But decisions about who is eligible vary based on official's interpretation of the criteria and ever shifting resettlement policies. Officials also must deal with cross-cultural differences and language barriers as they decide who is a refugee and who is an "economic refugee," or someone whose main motive to move is for economic advantage.

The Nuer who live in the U.S. have made it through this bureaucratic process. Thok Ding, for example, was brought up herding cattle in a pastoral village, suffered the death of his father when northerners attacked his village, moved with his family to a camp in Ethiopia, attended and excelled at a Christian mission school there, moved to another camp for further schooling, moved back to the Sudan with his family when fighting broke out in Ethiopia, traveled back to Addis Ababa where he joined friends, moved to a camp in Kenya, applied for refugee status with the UN there, and was eventually accepted for refugee resettlement by the U.S.

His arrival and settlement in the United States was facilitated by Lutheran Social Services, a voluntary organization ("volag" to insiders) contracted by the U.S. Helped by the organization, he was placed in Minneapolis, settled in an apartment, and guided toward a job. Later he left Minneapolis for Des Moines and a job in the meat packing industry, where he hopes to continue his education, save money, marry a woman from the Sudan, and bring his family, with whom he corresponds frequently and to whom he sends money, to the United States.

The case illustrates several points. Refugee issues are complex, varied, and involve endless bureaucratic hurdles. Refugees who manage to gain resettlement (many do not), must be tenacious, ambitious, cleaver, and opportunistic. The Nuer make successful refugees because many possess these characteristics.

QUESTIONS

True or False?

T   1.   According to Shandy (New Americans: The Road to Refugee Resettlement), Nuer refugees who have been resettled in the United States were originally a pastoral people living in the southern Sudan

F   2.   According to Shandy (New Americans: The Road to Refugee Resettlement), Nuer refugees have been sent to the United States by Christian missionaries who live in the southern Sudan.

F   3.   Shandy (New Americans: The Road to Refugee Resettlement) notes that the UN defines refugees as IDPs or "internally displaced persons."

T   4.   According to Shandy (New Americans: The Road to Refugee Resettlement), the first anthropologist to conduct and published extensive ethnography about the Nuer of the southern Sudan was Sir E. E. Evans-Pritchard.

T   5.   According to Shandy, (New Americans: The Road to Refugee Resettlement), the UN looks at three possible solutions to the refugee problem: voluntary repatriation to the country of origin, integration into a country of asylum, or third country resettlement.

F   6.   Shandy (New Americans: The Road to Refugee Resettlement) argues that the only way refugees can gain resettlement in another country is by having a useful skill needed by the country or by the intervention of relatives or friends who guarantee they will provide the refugees with jobs.

T   7.   According to Shandy (New Americans: The Road to Refugee Resettlement), Thok Ding was finally resettled in the U.S. after his father was killed in the Sudanese civil war, and he attended school in Ethiopia and lived in a refugee camp in Kenya.

F   8.   According to Shandy (New Americans: The Road to Refugee Resettlement), the UN has several categories of refugees. The refugee most likely to be accepted for resettlement in a second country is called the "economic refugee."

Multiple Choice

1. According to Shandy (New Americans: The Road to Refugee Resettlement) the UN classifies refugees as people with a well founded fear of persecution based on
    a.   race or religion.
    b.   membership in a particular social group.
    c.   political opinion.
    d.   two of the above.
    * e.   a, b, and c above.

2. According to Shandy (New Americans: The Road to Refugee Resettlement), the Nuer of southern Sudan were first studied by
    * a.   Sir E. E. Evans-Pritchard.
    b.   Sir Thok Ding.
    c.   Robert Gardner.
    d.   Sharon Hutchinson.
    e.   Marvin Harris.

3. Shandy (New Americans: The Road to Refugee Resettlement), notes that the civil war that has wracked the Sudan for years is often said by outsiders to be between
    a.   the Nuer and the Dinka.
    b.   northern Arabs and southern Africans.
    c.   northern Muslims and Southern Christians.
    * d.   two of the above.
    e.   a, b, and c above.

4. According to Shandy (New Americans: The Road to Refugee Resettlement), Nuer boys go through a painful initiation ceremony called the
    a.   IDP ceremony.
    * b.   gaar ceremony.
    c.   cicatrisation ceremony.
    d.   rite of passage.
    e.   ngoya ceremony.

5. According to Shandy (New Americans: The Road to Refugee Resettlement), Nuer are most often first aided in their resettled in the United States by
    a.   relatives.
    b.   UN officials.
    * c.   voluntary associations (volags).
    d.   friends.
    e.   U.S. immigration officials.

6. According to Shandy (New Americans: The Road to Refugee Resettlement), *transnationalism* is defined as
   a. the nationalistic fervor of one people that causes them to go to war with another.
   b. the shifting of national loyalties from one nation state to another.
   c. another word for global markets.
 * d. the cross-cutting ties that span the borders of nation-states.
   e. a political movement in the southern Sudan.

7. Shandy (New Americans: The Road to Refugee Resettlement), notes that the U.S. immigration service has settled the Nuer in about 30 different states because
   a. they could not find a single location for them all.
   b. they feel refugees adjust better if they are scattered in small groups around the country.
   c. they will have less of a negative impact on community if there are fewer of them.
 * d. two of the above.
   e. none of the above.

PART 7

LAW AND POLITICS

The introduction to Part 7 includes a discussion of basic concepts associated with the anthropology of law and politics.

KEY DEFINITIONS

An **infralegal dispute** is one that occurs outside the legal system without involving regular violence.

An **extralegal dispute** is one that occurs outside the law and escalates into violence.

Law is the cultural knowledge that people use to settle disputes by means of agents who have recognized authority to do so.

Self-redress is a legal process of dispute settlement where the disputants, themselves, are given the right to make settlement.

A **go-between** is a trusted third party who is given the Right to negotiate a dispute resolution.

An **ordeal** is a dispute resolution process that requires a disputant to take a powerful oath or submit to a (usually painful) test.

A **moot** is an informal community meeting with the right to settle disputes.

A **court** is a formal organization with the right to settle disputes.

The **political system** is the process of making and carrying out public policy according to cultural categories and rules.

Policy refers to guidelines for action.

Public refers to the group of people affected by policy.

Support is anything that contributes to the adoption and enforcement of public policy.

Legitimacy is a kind of support based on people's positive evaluation of public policy or public officials.

Coercion is support derived from the threat or use of force or the promise of short-term gain.

Authority is the right to make and enforce public policy.

Leadership is the ability to influence others to act.

QUESTIONS

True or False?

T   1.   Any guidelines that can lead directly to action are called "policy."

F   2.   A leader is a person who obtains power through authority.

F   3.   If a dictator forces people to adhere to his policies by using force, his actions would not fall under the definition of support.

T   4.   The process of making and carrying out public policy according to cultural categories and rules is called the political system.

T   5.   When the members of a society permit two people to settle a dispute by fighting each other, we call their action self-redress and classify it as part of the legal system.

T   6.   The primary means of gaining conformity and order from individual members of a society is through enculturation.

F   7.   A feud is a good example of a kind of support called coercion.

F   8.   According to anthropologists, all human disputes are dealt with by legal systems, not just ones that go to a formal court.

Multiple Choice

1. The cultural knowledge that people use to settle disputes by means of agents who have recognized authority is called
   * a.   law.
     b.   politics.
     c.   a court.
     d.   self-redress.
     e.   a moot.

2. A dispute that is below the level of the legal process is a(n)
    a. legal dispute.
    b. extra legal dispute.
  * c. infralegal dispute.
    d. feud.
    e. war.

3. A feud is an example of
    a. coercion.
    b. self-redress.
    c. a legal dispute.
    d. an infralegal dispute.
  * e. an extralegal dispute.

4. When disputes are settled through a community meeting that provides for an informal airing of the conflict, we term this kind of settlement process a(n)
    a. ordeal.
    b. self-redress.
    c. court.
  * d. moot.
    e. contest.

5. The right to make and enforce public policy is called
    a. coercion.
  * b. authority.
    c. support.
    d. legitimacy.
    e. leadership.

6. The people whom a policy will affect are called the
  * a. public.
    b. faction.
    c. state.
    d. tribe.
    e. band.

7. Anything that contributes to the adoption of public policy and its enforcement is called
    a. authority.
    b. coercion.
    c. legitimacy.
  * d. support.
    e. leadership.

8. When people feel that a policy is wrong, but accept it because they value the government that makes the policy, they are giving a kind of support called
    * a. legitimacy.
    b. coercion.
    c. authority.
    d. leadership.
    e. self-redress.

9. Which one of the following has **not** been used by at least one society as a legal structure for settling disputes?
    a. moot
    b. go-between
    c. ordeal
    d. self-redress
    * e. none of the above

10. The process of making and carrying out public policy through the use of culturally defined categories and rules is called
    * a. the political system.
    b. legitimacy.
    c. coercion.
    d. the infra legal system.
    e. authority.

Article 29

Law and Order   JAMES P. SPRADLEY AND DAVID W. McCURDY

Summary In this article, Spradley and McCurdy present law in the context of dispute resolution, using trouble cases drawn from anthropologist Laura Nader's work in Ralu'a, a Zapotec Indian village located in southern Mexico. The piece begins with Nader's arrival in Ralu'a and describes an ongoing dispute over the use of washing stones at the village well between two women. The dispute was settled when the *presidente* (village chairman who also presides over the village court) and other elected village officials formed a work force, improved the washing facilities at the well, and declared that washing stones would no longer be owned by individuals. The rest of the article deals with several concepts—the structure of legal culture including substantive law and procedural law, legal levels, legal principles and cultural values. Substantive law consists of the legal statutes that define right and wrong. This is illustrated in the article by the flirtation of a married man with a married woman, which the Zapotec treat as a crime. Similarly, the case of a son who struck his father is also defined as a crime to be dealt with by the community's legal system. Procedural law refers to the agreed upon ways to settle disputes. In Ralu'a, for example, one should not take family disputes to court (although on some occasions the court will be forced to hear them) but disputes between villagers such as the argument over the washing stone, should be taken to court if they cannot be settled between the disputing individuals beforehand. Legal systems also reflect legal principles and cultural values. For the Zapotec, a major legal principle is to "make the balance," meaning to encourage compromise and settlement so that disputes disappear and disputants get along with each other in the future. This in turn is based on the Zapotec cultural value of maintaining social equilibrium. A direct confrontation between individuals where one loses and another wins is unsettling to community members.

QUESTIONS

True or False?

F.   1   Spradley and McCurdy (Law and Order) argue that a key to maintaining order in the tightly knit Zapotec community of Ralu'a is the strict application of law and punishment by village officials.

F   2.   According to Spradley and McCurdy (Law and Order), substantive law is codified in writing in literate societies. In nonliterate societies, people define what a crime is by using procedural law.

T   3.   According to Spradley and McCurdy (Law and Order), there is no substantive law that prohibits a man from beating his wife in the Zapotec village of Ralu'a..

T   4.   According to Spradley and McCurdy (Law and Order), a legal principle for the people who live in Ralu'a is "*hacer el balance*," to make the balance.

F 5. According to Spradley and McCurdy (Law and Order), a legal principle is defined as an agreed upon way to settle a dispute.

T 6. According to Spradley and McCurdy (Law and Order), in the Zapotec village of Ralu'a, frightening someone so that they come down with *susto* or magical fright, is a crime.

F 7. According to Spradley and McCurdy (Law and Order), the system of legal levels in the Zapotec village of Ralu'a means that disputes can only be settled by the *presidente* or *principales*.

Multiple Choice

1. According to Spradley and McCurdy (Law and Order), in the Zapotec village of Ralu'a two married people were fined for flirting with each other by the presidente. The prohibition on flirting is an example of
    * a. substantive law.
    b. procedural law.
    c. a legal principle.
    d. infralegal law.
    e. extralegal law.

2. According to Spradley and McCurdy (Law and Order), the agreed upon ways to settle disputes are called
    a. courts.
    b. legal principles.
    * c. procedural law.
    d. substantive law.
    e. self redress.

3. Spradley and McCurdy (Law and Order) argue that the legal statues that define right and wrong are called
    a. legal rules.
    b. substantive law.
    * c. procedural law.
    d. legal levels.
    e. legal principles.

4. According to Spradley and McCurdy (Law and Order), the rule in Ralu'a that *principales* and their families should not use the court to settle family disputes is an example of
    a. self redress.
    b. legal levels.
    c. legal structure.
    * d. procedural law.
    e. substantive law.

5. As reported by Spradley and McCurdy (Law and Order), anthropologist Laura Nader feels that in Ralu'a, there is a strong value on _____, which underlies the community's substantive and procedural law.
   a. private property
   b. religious piety
   c. personal success
   d. hard work
   * e. maintaining equilibrium

6. According to Spradley and McCurdy (Law and Order), toward the end of her stay in Ralu'a, anthropologists Laura Nader "made the balance," by
   a. convincing the priest that she was not a protestant.
   b. working as a *mayoral* in the court.
   * c. donating a barrel of *mescal* at a fiesta.
   d. giving gifts to the *presidente* and other town officials.
   e. donating money to build a new washing area.

Article 30

Cross-Cultural Law:
The Case of the Gypsy Offender

ANNE SUTHERLAND

Summary This article by Anne Sutherland looks at what happens when members of one society live under the legal jurisdiction of another. The article describes the case of a nineteen-year-old Gypsy accused of using someone else's social security number and the role played by an anthropologist in his defense.

The case came out of the actions of the young Gypsy male who used the social security number of a five-year-old nephew to apply for a car loan. Although he had no intention of stealing the car or defrauding anyone, the man was charged under a new law that makes it a felony to use someone else's social security number. The police also searched his apartment, where they found a longer list of names and social security numbers, concluding that he was part of a car theft ring.

Sutherland became involved in the case as an expert witness for the defense. Her first act was to discover whether the young man was a Gypsy and what his name was. Gypsies take on many "American" names, which they change often. Their identity more typically is associated with their *vitsa*, or clan, and a larger grouping of clans called a *natsia*. She was able to identify his kinship identities and later to explain Gypsy identity patterns in court.

During the trial she testified that the young man had no intention of defrauding or stealing from anyone. She noted that it was usual for members of *vitsas* to share things, including names, social security numbers, and other marks of identity. Despite her testimony, the defendant was convicted.

Sutherland concludes her article with three points. First, Gypsies, who are a nomadic group, do not stress individual identities, which are so important to settled Americans. For hundreds of years Gypsies have been persecuted by the people and governments of the countries in which they live. She cites ample evidence that American police also consider them a criminal society. Hiding their identity has been their response to this persecution. Second, Gypsies suffer to an unusual extent in jail because they believe they are polluted there. Gypsies avoid long contact with non-Gypsies because the latter pollute (make *marime*) them. They are shunned by their own relatives if this happens and must go through a period of purification and reintegration into their own society. In addition, they cannot eat jail food without being polluted by it. They can eat food that is wrapped or packaged in containers, and one of the first things that Sutherland did was to see that the young Gypsy man could receive wrapped food in jail (he had lost 15 pounds before his trial). Third, there is a clash between the Gypsy view of membership in a corporate kin group and the usual American view of individual rights. In short, Gypsies believe that the *vitsa* has rights over property such as names and social security numbers and that *vitsa* members can share in these things. In the end, Sutherland notes, Gypsies will have to accept that what is perfectly normal to them is a crime in the United States.

QUESTIONS

True or False?

T   1.   Sutherland (The Case of the Gypsy Offender), presents the description of a legal case where a nineteen-year-old Gypsy boy is convicted of using someone else's social security number despite the fact that he had no intention of defrauding anyone.

T   2.   According to Sutherland (The Case of the Gypsy Offender), Gypsies frequently take one another's social security numbers in order to hide their identity.

F   3.   Sutherland (The Case of the Gypsy Offender) describes a case in which a young Gypsy man was falsely accused of fraud by police in St. Paul, Minnesota.

F   4.   According to Sutherland, the largest group to which Gypsies belong is called the *vitsa*.

T   5.   Sutherland argues that Gypsies hide their personal identity as a way to combat persecution by members of the societies in which they live.

F   6.   Sutherland notes that the young Gypsy man she helped to defend in court refused to eat jail food as a protest for not being allowed to call his relatives.

Multiple Choice

1.   According to Sutherland (The Case of the Gypsy Offender), a young Gypsy man was indicted by the government for
    a.   hiding his identity from authorities.
    b.   stealing cars.
  * c.   using a relative's social security number.
    d.   refusing to eat jail food.
    e.   lying to authorities about his real American name.

2.   Sutherland (The Case of the Gypsy Offender) notes that the lawyer defending a young Gypsy man of using a relative's social security number argued in court that
  * a.   the Gypsy had not intended to commit a crime when he used the number.
    b.   the Gypsy used the number because of a fear of pollution (*marime*) from non-Gypsies.
    c.   Gypsies did not traditionally use social security so social security numbers had no importance to them.
    d.   two of the above.
    e.   none of the above.

3. According to Sutherland (the Case of the Gypsy Offender), Gypsies treat social security numbers as
   a. unimportant, since they don't use social security.
 * b. corporate property of their kin group, the *vitsa*.
   c. a way to defraud banks so that they can get illegal loans.
   d. a source of prestige, since they believe higher numbers bring greater success.
   e. something to be traded among themselves for cash.

4. Sutherland reports that for Gypsies, going to jail
   a. often provides needed time to recover from alcoholism.
   b. helps them learn English and skills that facilitate getting real jobs in American society.
   c. is welcomed because they finally get enough to eat there.
 * d. is an especially cruel punishment because it separates them from their kin.
   e. is hard on them because they are targeted by other inmates as easy prey.

5. The case of the Gypsy defendant described by Sutherland represents a good illustration of what happens when
   a. a foreign people takes advantage of a lenient judicial system.
   b. police exceed the law in their eagerness to fight crime.
   c. greedy lawyers misrepresent their non-American clients.
   d. anthropological testimony is misused in court.
 * e. a normal practice for one group is a crime for another.

6. According to Sutherland (The Case of the Offender), Gypsies find which of the following things polluting (*marime*)?
   a. relatives from other *vitsas*.
   b. non-Gypsies.
   c. food prepared by non-Gypsies that is not in some sort of package or container.
 * d. two of the above.
   e. a, b, and c above.

7. According to Sutherland, officials in the American justice system often
 * a. view Gypsies as a criminal society.
   b. trump up evidence against Gypsies.
   c. deny Gypsy defendants their rights while they are in jail.
   d. two of the above.
   e. all of the above.

Article 31

Life Without Chiefs

MARVIN HARRIS

Summary In this article, Marvin Harris traces the evolution of political systems and refutes the idea that human beings are biologically wired to form hierarchies and formal political structures. Instead, culture, especially economic structures and the size of societies, affects what political systems will look like, not inheritance. Can people exist without some people ruling and others being ruled? The answer is yes if we look at hunting and gathering societies, the condition under which most of our biological evolution occurred. Hunter/gatherers have no formal leaders. They live in small bands where delayed reciprocity is the economic rule. Generosity is expected; people share equally. There are no goods or resources to control and to make people dependent on someone. As a result, there are no formal leaders although influential people, like U.S. scoutmasters, can lead by example. Such people may be called "headmen" but they cannot command others to do anything. If band members don't like something, they can simply leave and visit another band.

As societies grow larger they may develop redistributive exchange. People turn over food and/or goods to a central figure for redistribution. Typically, to maintain a position of prestige, such "big men" will have to give more than they receive. But in time, as agriculture grows in importance and societies further increase in size, people come to big men for support and he, in turn, can call on them to produce things for redistribution. His prestige grows and people eventually view his status as an office, making him a chief. Chiefs possess more authority to command action and gain material possessions. Eventually chiefdoms evolve into states, and states into empires.

QUESTIONS

True or False

T   1.   According to Harris (Life without Chiefs), hunter/gathers had no formal leaders. Instead there were headmen who were respected people but who had no authority to command anyone to do anything.

F   2.   According to Harris (Life without Chiefs), leaders called "big men" appear in societies characterized by delayed reciprocity.

T   3.   According to Harris (Life without Chiefs), social stratification gained momentum wherever extra food produced by the "inspired diligence of redistributors" could be stored in anticipation of redistributions.

F   4.   Harris (Life without Chiefs) notes that big men, because of their position as redistributors, tend to amass more wealth and live in more comfort than other people in their societies.

T   5.   According to Harris (Life without Chiefs), the hierarchy and leaders with authority arise in human society as a result of culture, especially economic factors and group size, not biological inheritance.

F   6.   According to Harris (Life without Chiefs), big men amassed more wealth than common people due to their position as redistributors.

T   7.   According to Harris (Life without Chiefs), The Cherokee living in what now is the state of Tennessee had a chiefdomship marked by a paramount chief and subordinate chiefs. Each Cherokee family had a corn crib, called " the chief's granary," in its fields where the grain was stored for the chief to redistribute.

Multiple Choice

1. In his article entitled "Life without Chiefs," Harris argues that _____ appear in conjunction with _____ exchange
    a.   big men: reciprocal
*   b.   big men: redistributive
    c.   headmen: redistributive
    d.   chiefs: reciprocal
    e.   presidents: market

2. According to Harris (Life without Chiefs), headmen
    a.   are found primarily in hunting and gathering societies.
    b.   become a center for the redistribution of food.
    c.   lead by example without authority.
*   d.   two of the above.
    e.   a, b, and c above.

3. According to Harris (Life Without Chiefs), *mumis,* or big men, among the Siuai of the Solomon Islands
    a.   possessed formal authority to make people act.
    b.   managed band reciprocity.
    c.   led in a manner equivalent to a "U.S. scoutmaster."
*   d.   ate less well than other people.
    e.   none of the above.

4. Harris (Life Without Chiefs) argues that
    a.   people inherit a tendency to form dominance hierarchies in their social groups.
    b.   all groups must be led by formal, clearly identifiable leaders with authority.
    c.   big men amassed more wealth than common people because of their position as redistributors.
    d.   nation states should adopt the political systems of our democratic ancestors, the hunter/gatherers.
*   e.   Chiefs could amass wealth and even inherit their formal position.

5. According to Harris (Life Without Chiefs) hunter/gatherers lack leaders with formal authority because
    * a. band members are not economically dependent on any one person in such societies.
    b. band members have not discovered the benefits of a formal political system.
    c. the economic importance of women makes it impossible for men to permanently acquire political authority.
    d. two of the above.
    e. none of the above.

6. According to Harris (Life Without Chiefs), the movement toward greater social stratification in human societies was inspired by
    a. the human tendency to form hierarchies.
    * b. the production of extra (beyond the immediate needs of people) food.
    c. the advent of formal religion.
    d. the fact that some men and some women produced more food than others.
    e. none of the above.

PART 8

RELIGION, MAGIC, AND WORLD VIEW

The introduction to Part 8 presents the reader with a number of concepts related to religious belief, action, and structure.

KEY DEFINITIONS

Religion is the cultural knowledge of the supernatural that people use to cope with the ultimate problems of human existence.

Supernatural refers to the realm beyond people's normal experience.

Ultimate problems include life's meaning, death, evil, and transcendent values.

Transcendent values are values that override people's individual goals and desires.

Personified supernatural force is supernatural power that resides in supernatural beings, such as deities, ghosts, and other kinds of spirits.

Mana is impersonal supernatural force that is free-floating and capable of inhabiting many different things.

Magic refers to the strategies that people use to control supernatural force to gain a desired end.

Sorcery is the malevolent use of magic.

Witchcraft labels the activities of people who possess, often without knowing it, supernatural power that is used for evil purposes.

A **prayer** is a petition directed at a supernatural being.

Sacrifice refers to the act of giving up something valuable to influence supernatural beings.

Spirit possession occurs when a supernatural being enters an individual and controls that person's behavior.

Divination is the use of supernatural force associated with material objects to provide answers to particular questions.

Shamans are religious specialists who control supernatural power.

Priests are religious specialists who mediate between people and the supernatural.

World view refers to a system of concepts and often unstated assumptions about life. It often contains a cosmology and mythology.

Cosmology refers to the cultural views about the nature of the world.

Mythology refers to the cultural views about how the world came to be the way it is.

Revitalization movements refer, in the words of A. F. C. Wallace, to "deliberate, organized, conscious efforts by members of a society to construct a more satisfying culture."

QUESTIONS

True or False?

T   1.   Religion helps people cope with such ultimate problems of their existence as the meaning of life, death, evil, and transcendent values.

F   2.   The term "supernatural" labels people's irrational beliefs about power in inanimate objects.

T   3.   If a religious specialist were to use a powerful saying to cure a sick individual, we would label him or her a shaman.

F   4.   If a person uses a powerful spell to hurt another individual, we would label him or her a witch.

T   5.   If a person believes that some rocks lying in a yam field contribute to the rapid growth of the plants, we might suspect the presence of a belief in mana.

F   6.   Stories about how the world came to be are called cosmology.

Multiple Choice

1. The cultural knowledge of the supernatural that people use to cope with the ultimate problems of human existence is called
    a.   personified supernatural power.
    b.   mana.
    c.   taboo.
    d.   transcendental values.
    * e.   religion.

2. Folk concepts of ghosts, spirits, ancestral beings, and gods are, according to most anthropologists, signs of belief in
    * a.   the supernatural.
    b.   taboo.
    c.   magic.
    d.   impersonal supernatural force.
    e.   sacrifice.

3. In some societies, people believe that individuals are born with supernatural force that they consciously or unconsciously use to cause harm. Anthropologists classify these supposed activities as
    a.   magic.
    b.   sorcery.
    * c.   witchcraft.
    d.   two of the above.
    e.   none of the above.

4. When someone uses a set of well-defined procedures to control and manipulate supernatural force in order to gain some end, he or she is practicing
    a.   prayer.
    * b.   magic.
    c.   witchcraft.
    d.   transcendent religion.
    e.   taboo.

5. Religious specialists who mediate between people and the supernatural are called
    a.   witches.
    b.   shamans.
    c.   diviners.
    * d.   priests.
    e.   witch doctors.

6. If a religious specialist reads the cracks in the burned scapula (shoulder blade) of a sheep in order to predict future events, the act would be called
   * a. divination.
   b. sorcery.
   c. magic.
   d. witchcraft.
   e. sacrifice.

7. Religious specialists who control supernatural power are called
   a. priests.
   b. diviners.
   * c. shamans.
   d. witch doctors.
   e. gurus.

Article 32

Taraka's Ghost   STANLEY A FREED AND RUTH S. FREED

Summary In this article, Stanley and Ruth Freed describe the possession of a village woman, Sita, by the ghost of a relative named Taraka. Diagnosing it as an altered psychological state, the Freeds show how possession is brought about by stress associated with Sita's encounters with sex and death as she was growing up.

Sita was first possessed in the 1950s when she was newly married. Criticized for working a sewing machine, she grew cold and collapsed. Later spectators determined that she was possessed by her dead cousin, Taraka. Sita's father engaged two exorcists, but their attempts to drive the ghost out of Sita failed.

Belief in ghosts is common in North India. Normally when people die, their souls are judged after 13 days to determine how they will be reborn. But souls of people who die badly or when they are unhappy may become ghosts. Ghosts can seize peoples' souls and hurt or kill their human hosts. Ghosts often possess (enter and at times control) people who were close to them in life. Taraka had become pregnant and committed suicide when her father asked her to kill herself, which deeply affected Sita. Two other of Sita's friends also died during her childhood and she associated their deaths with sex and childbirth. When she joined her new husband, she refused to have sex with him for some time. When the marriage was finally consummated, Sita began to experience possession by Taraka's ghost. The stress of leaving home and having sexual relations was probably the cause.

Marriage is a difficult time for young women in India. Most move from the support of their natal families to a restricted life in their husband's home. Brides often experience ghost possession in India, indicating that possession is linked to stress. Psychologists argue that stress causes the body to produce endorphins that relieve pain but may trigger altered states. Ghost possession can be understood as one of these states.

The article concludes by tracing events in Sita's later years—her nine pregnancies, an abortion, miscarriages, and the deaths of several lactose intolerant babies. During this time, the treatments for ghost possession gave her apparent protection against Taraka's ghost and relieved her anxiety. Stress was reduced and when last seen she was a leader among the women of her family.

QUESTIONS

True or False?

F   1.   According to the Freeds (Taraka's Ghost), North Indian women are often possessed by the Ghosts of unfortunate male lovers.

124

T   2.   The Freeds (Taraka's Ghost) argue that malevolent spirit possession in North India is often associated with high levels of stress.

F   3.   According to the Freeds (Taraka's Ghost), Sita's father and husband were embarrassed by her ghost possession and usually kept her secluded during her seizures.

T   4.   According to the Freeds (Taraka's Ghost), women are most likely to be possessed by ghosts when they are first married and separated from their family of birth.

F   5.   The Freeds (Taraka's Ghost) described how a young Indian woman, Sita, was possessed by the Ghost of a woman who committed suicide after sleeping with Sita's new husband.

T   6.   According to the Freeds (Taraka's Ghost) Sita's possession by Taraka, her dead cousin, was connected to her anxiety about sex and death.

Multiple Choice

1.   According to the Freeds (Taraka's Ghost), ghost spirit possession of women in North India is associated with
      a.   overwork.
  *   b.   stress.
      c.   tensions among members of her natal family.
      d.   competition among peers.
      e.   malnutrition.

2.   The Freeds (Taraka's Ghost) note that stress increases for Indian women at the time of their marriage because
      a.   they move from the freedom of their parent's home to restrictions of their husband's household.
      b.   their kin (fathers, mothers, brothers, and sisters) are considered inferior by their husbands' relatives.
      c.   they rank low when they enter their husbands' households for the first time.
      d.   two of the above.
  *   e.   a, b, and c above.

3.   According to the Freeds (Taraka's Ghost), Sita
  *   a.   associated death with sex and childbirth.
      b.   cured her anxieties over sex and childbirth through the help of her friend, Taraka.
      c.   was quickly cured of ghost possession by an exorcist hired by her father.
      d.   only endured ghost possession when she went home to visit her mother and father.
      e.   was raped by a school teacher when she was 13 year old.

4. According to the Freeds (Taraka's Ghost),
   a. when people die, their souls become wandering ghosts for at least 11 years.
   b. ghosts are often released from their restless state in India after they are deemed to have done a good deed for someone.
   c. ghosts are usually the souls of strangers who invade people's lives and communities.
 * d. ghosts are the souls of people who die too young and in an unfortunate way, or who were unhappy in life.
   e. none of the above.

5. According to the Freeds (Taraka's Ghost), Taraka's ghost was the soul of Sita's
 * a. cousin who had committee suicide after becoming pregnant.
   b. mother who had lived an unhappy life and died of pneumonia.
   c. friend who had been raped by a schoolmaster.
   d. father, who was killed during the Second World War serving in the British army.
   e. uncle, who was murdered by his lover's jealous husband.

6. According to examples presented by the Freeds (Taraka's Ghost), in North India ghosts can
   a. live in wells.
   b. possess women who were their friends in life.
   c. seize people's souls and hurt or kill them.
 * d. two of the above.
   e. a, b, and c above.

Article 33

Baseball Magic

GEORGE GMELCH

Summary This updated selection by George Gmelch shows how Americans use magical ritual to reduce the anxiety associated with uncertainty. Gmelch focuses on the magic of baseball players. Citing the work of Bronislaw Malinowski on magic, he describes how ritual surrounds two of the three main activities associated with the game, hitting and pitching. This is because both involve uncertainty. Fielding, the other activity, is relatively error-free and receives little magical attention. Baseball players display most varieties of magic. They use personal magic, such as a regular cap adjustment before each pitch; fetishes, such as lucky pennies; special diets; special clothing; and a host of other devices they feel are associated with successful play. They also carry fetishes and observe taboos, including the one against crossing bats.

At the root of such behavior is the notion that people associate things with each other that have no functional relationship. If a pitcher eats pancakes for breakfast and wins a game that day, he may continue to eat them each time he plays because the act is now associated with success on the field. Citing research on rats and pigeons, Gmelch notes that once an association is established, it only takes sporadic success to perpetuate the relationship.

Gmelch concludes that although they do not attribute their acts to any special supernatural power, baseball players nonetheless follow magical practices carefully to ensure luck and guard against failure.

QUESTIONS

True or False?

F   1.   Gmelch argues that magic is found most often associated with fielding in American baseball.

T   2.   Baseball players often include personal ritual, taboos, and fetishes in their practice of magic.

F   3.   Skinner explains magic as a response to uncertainty, an attempt to control the unpredictable, according to Gmelch.

T   4.   According to Gmelch, magical ritual is most often associated with hitting and pitching in baseball.

F   5.   Pitchers have the most control over the outcome of what they do in baseball and therefore use the least magic.

T   6.   Gmelch quotes a theory by anthropologist Bronislaw Malinowski that argues for the association between magic and uncertainty.

Multiple Choice

1.   Magic, according to Malinowski (cited in "Baseball Magic"), occurs in response to
    a.   anger.
    b.   frustration.
 * c.   anxiety.
    d.   social pressure.
    e.   none of the above.

2.   The baseball activity over which players have the least control, according to Gmelch, is
 * a.   pitching.
    b.   hitting.
    c.   fielding.
    d.   bench warming.
    e.   arguing with the umpire.

3.   According to Skinner, as noted by Gmelch, once established, magic requires _____ to be maintained.
    a.   regular rewards
 * b.   sporadic rewards
    c.   formal instruction
    d.   uncertainty
    e.   all of the above

4.   Gmelch notes that during one season when he was playing baseball, he refrained from eating pancakes. This is an example of what anthropologists call
    a.   a fetish.
 * b.   a taboo.
    c.   mana.
    d.   charms.
    e.   a ritual.

5.   Gmelch notes that fetishes are often associated with baseball magic. These are
    a.   things to be avoided.
    b.   repetitive actions.
 * c.   sacred objects.
    d.   sayings.
    e.   aquatic animals with fins.

6. A magical practice in baseball that is culturally learned rather than personal, is
   a. the wearing of the lucky number, 77.
   b. wearing a pair of shoes that bring luck.
   c. tugging the hat before each pitch.
   d. placing a penny for each win in one's athletic supporter cup.
 * e. mentioning a no-hitter while the game is in progress.

Article 34

Witchcraft Tswana Style CHARLANNE BURKE

Summary In this article, Charlanne Burke describes the persistence and ongoing function of witchcraft beliefs in modern Botswana. Once a pervasive view of how adversity was caused, witchcraft beliefs continue in slightly altered form to explain not only traditional problems such as illness, but more recent adversities such as low exam grades and inability to find work.

Using two cases, one from 1933 and the other from 1997, Burke introduces an historical Tswana distinction between "medicine killing" and "malevolent magic." Today's witchcraft revolves largely around the latter. Anthropologists usually define witchcraft as the supernatural ability of one person to hurt another and as an internal, inherited, often unconscious state. Sorcery, on the other hand, is the malevolent act of manipulating special powers and materials to hurt others. The Batswana system of witchcraft beliefs might better be classified as sorcery because people believe individuals actually use power to hurt others. However, such acts are rarely, if ever, witnessed. The Batswana also conceive of two kinds of witches. There are night witches, women who are thought to kill their own family members to gain evil power. They are associated with owls, bats, and cats, causing people to be wary of these animals. Day witches, the most common kind, are ordinary men and women who use herbs and other "medicines" procured from healers to hurt people. Unlike the past, today there are few public accusations of witchcraft. People defend against witches, who are usually women and usually believed to be kin, friends, or neighbors, by using medicines and rituals provided by healers, visiting the hospital if disease is the problem, or enlisting the aid of church officials and congregations.

Burke's research centered on young people in Botswana, so her information about witchcraft is youth centered. She learned that young people are not thought to practice witchcraft because they lack the proper knowledge, but they can be empowered by witches to hurt people. Young people feel that witchcraft can cause dizziness, headaches, eye problems, back and abdominal pain, blindness, inability to speak, inability to read or hold things, infertility, and insanity. AIDS is often attributed to witchcraft. The work of witches is illustrated by the experience of Ofaletse, a young woman who assisted Burke in the field. She believed that a neighbor, Sophie, was jealous of her and hurt her family and children, and curtailed her ability to find work. To combat the witchcraft, she has gone to healers and later, a church congregation. Burke concludes that despite modern education, witchcraft beliefs persist among the Batswana because they explain adversity and give people a way to combat it.

QUESTIONS

True or False?

F 1. According to Burke (Witchcraft Tswana Style), a new witchcraft has emerged in Botswana involving the use of incantations by witches, who send them in letters to their victims

T 2. Burke (Witchcraft Tswana Style) notes that the people of Botswana believe that witches can cause AIDS.

F 3. According to Burke (Witchcraft Tswana Style), most witches today are classified as "night witches" and hurt other people by using powerful incantations against them.

T 4. Burke (Witchcraft Tswana Style) writes that most people think that kin, neighbors, and even friends are mostly likely to be the witches attacking them.

F 5. Burke (Witchcraft Tswana Style) argues that Botswana witches do not fit the usual anthropological definition of witchcraft because they are born with evil power and may not even know they have it.

T 6. According to Burke (Witchcraft Tswana Style), Batswana believe that witches can cause dizziness, headaches, eye problems, back and abdominal pain, blindness, inability to speak or hold things, inability to read, infertility, and insanity, among others.

F 7. Burke (Witchcraft Tswana Style) argues that today's witchcraft in Botswana is a holdover from the past and is weakening as a belief system.

T 8. Burke (Witchcraft Tswana Style) describes the beliefs of a woman named Ofaletse who feels that a neighbor is causing her and her family to be ill and have bad luck

Multiple Choice

1. According to Burke (Witchcraft Tswana Style), modern witches are divided into two kinds by Batswana. These are
    a. killer magicians and night witches.
  * b. night witches and day witches.
    c. sorcerers and magicians.
    d. voodoo and vodun witches.
    e. light and dark witches.

131

2. Burke (Witchcraft Tswana Style) argues that witchcraft beliefs in Botswana
  * a. function to explain adversity and provide ways for people to deal with it.
    b. are a survival from the past that have little function in today's world.
    c. are blamed on jealous strangers.
    d. have nearly disappeared because they conflict with modern notions of the world.
    e. are rejected by most educated Batswana.

3. According to Burke (Witchcraft Tswana Style), witches are thought to cause
    a. AIDS.
    b. the death of cats, owls, and bats.
    c. pens to write wrong exam answers.
  * d. two of the above.
    e. a, b, and c above.

4. According to Burke (Witchcraft Tswana Style), anthropologists traditional defined witchcraft as the supernatural ability of one person to hurt another that
    a. is taught to them by older witches using a complex code of spells, medicines, and familiars.
    b. involves the actual use of magic.
  * c. is internal and often an inherited unconscious power that witches may not know they have.
    d. is socially rejected as inappropriate.
    e. none of the above.

5. According to Burke (Witchcraft Tswana Style), Ofaletse believed that a _____ was bewitching her.
    a. school friend.
    b. sister.
    c. brother.
  * d. neighbor
    e. stranger from another village.

6. Burke (Witchcraft Tswana Style) notes that today, Batswana deal with witchcraft
    a. by taking accused witches to government court.
    b. by enlisting the aid of healers who may use medicines to ward off witches.
    c. by enlisting the aid of church congregations and leaders to ward off the evil worked by witches.
  * d. two of the above.
    e. none of the above.

Article 35

Cargo Beliefs and Religious Experience   STEPHEN C. LEAVITT

Summary Revitalization movements (see the introduction to Part 9 for a description) take many forms, but none seem more unusual than the cargo cults of New Guinea. (Cargo is pigeon for Western goods.) In this article, Stephen Leavitt describes New Guinea cargo movements, reviews some of the theories developed to explain them, and adds his own interpretation of cargo beliefs based on his fieldwork among the Bumbita Arapesh of Papua New Guinea.

Cargo cults have occurred again and again in New Guinea. They involve attempts, usually through ritual, to attain vast amounts of material wealth thought to be under the control of ancestral spirits. When Europeans first arrived in New Guinea, people there were amazed at the wealth of goods they unloaded from their ships. Cargo movements arose to explain this miraculous wealth. Cult leaders would tell people that Europeans acquired cargo by performing special rituals. They believed that if native peoples performed these rituals, they, too, would receive cargo from the ancestors. Rituals often took the form of endless praying, hymn singing, and marching in lines, all things local people had seen Europeans doing. In some cases, people even built airstrips where planes could land with cargo or jetties where cargo-laden ships could dock. The Bumbita had such a movement in 1971 when a prophet, Yaliwan, claimed that the removal of two cement survey markers from the top of a well-known mountain would permit cargo to emerge. Among the Bumbit today the term "cargo cults" is held in bad repute by most people but a longing for cargo persists.

Anthropologists classify cargo cults as revitalization movements, and argue that they have occurred in response to colonial rule. Cults emphasize ritual, the visions of prophets, and a complete transformation of the world. What is unique about them, however, is their focus on the acquisition of cargo and the association of cargo with ancestors. Many anthropologists assert that these unique features reflect traditional culture; in the past people felt it was largely their ancestors who watched after them. Traditional culture also emphasized the gift giving as a way to build relationships and achieve prestige. For them sharing goods was paramount, yet Europeans who were now a powerful part of their social worlds and who had such wonderful goods, would not establish relationships by sharing their goods. Cargo, argued anthropologists, was the key to achieve greater equality with Europeans and to enhance native prestige. Ancestors were the logical source of cargo for the living.

Leavitt argues that this explanation is only part of the story because, although the People of New Guinea know where Western goods come from, cargo beliefs persist. Basing his analysis on the narratives of two Bumbita men, Leavitt asserts that the giving of cargo by dead parents or grand parents (ancestors) also serves as a sign of forgiveness and support for the living. In one case he reports that Matthew, a sixty-year-old man, felt that his father's spirit was now inside a missionary who had given him a gift. The gift was a sign of forgiveness by his father for the unpleasantness of a dispute they had had when Matthew was young.

John, a second, older man, felt God was his father and that God communicated to him through dreams. In one dream he sees piles of cargo and in another God indicates He will give him a high position in heaven. For John, both dreams are signs of support and forgiveness. They reveal visions of splendid cargo, awe of the power of older generations, a sense of being right with God, and finally, that God is really his own father. In this interpretation, cargo beliefs are much more than a simple desire for Western goods.

Leavitt concludes by saying that Bumbita face their changing and bewildering world and future by couching it in familiar personal family relationships. Cargo is a sign that the supportive spirits are really there.

QUESTIONS

True or False?

T 1. According to Leavitt (Cargo Beliefs and Religious Experience), cargo cults are revitalization movements that involve attempts, usually through ritual, to attain material wealth thought to be under the control of ancestral spirits.

F 2. Leavitt (Cargo Beliefs and Religious Experience) notes that when he went to New Guinea to study cargo cults in 1984, he discovered that there were no longer any movements to be observed.

T. 3. According to Leavitt, a Bumbita leader named Yaliwan prophesied that if people removed two cement survey markers from the top of a nearby mountain, the mountain would yield vast amounts of western goods (cargo).

F 4. According to Leavitt, cargo cults are different from other revitalization movements because they focus on ancestors as the source of western goods, rather than on God or other powerful supernatural beings.

T 5. According to Leavitt, anthropologists have explained the focus on ancestors and cargo in New Guinea by suggesting they fit with preexisting belief in the supportive intervention of ancestors and the power that the exchange of goods gave to people as they established relationships and sought prestige.

F 6. Leavitt (Cargo Beliefs and Religious Experience) argues that cargo beliefs have continued in New Guinea despite the fact that most people have converted to Christianity and no longer believe in the existence of their ancestors.

T 7. In his article, "Cargo Beliefs and Religious Experience," Leavitt relates a narrative given by a Bumbita man named Matthew in which Matthew sees the reincarnation of his father in a missionary who gives him a gift of salt.

F   8.   In his article, "Cargo Beliefs and Religious Experience," Leavitt relates a narrative told by a Bumbita man named John who, in dreams, is shown that God will encourage John's dead father to come back and give John cargo.

T   9.   According to Leavitt (Cargo Beliefs and Religious Experience), it is important to understand religion in terms of how individuals use it to explain and support their own lives.

Multiple Choice

1.   A central point that Leavitt makes about cargo beliefs (Cargo Beliefs and Religious Experience) among the Bumbita based on narratives given by two male informants, is that such beliefs must be understood in terms of
  * a.   a need for signs of support from deceased parents or grandparents.
     b.   Christian teachings about sin and redemption.
     c.   the pressure missionaries placed on the men to convert to Christianity.
     d.   the appeal of western machinery to Bumbita men..
     e.   the importance of missionaries as a source of financial support.

2.   According to Leavitt (Cargo Beliefs and Religious Experience), cargo cults are
     a.   Christian sects.
  * b.   revitalization movements.
     c.   the original religion of New Guinea peoples.
     d.   religious movements based on a belief in the sanctity of ships.
     e.   political revolutions aimed at the overthrow of current governments.

3.   Leavitt (Cargo Beliefs and Religious Experience) notes that over the decades, New Guinea cargo cults have taken the form of
     a.   copying the ritual behaviors of Europeans, such as missionaries and colonial officials.
     b.   building airstrips with bamboo control towers.
     c.   collecting money with which to buy American President Lyndon Johnson.
     d.   marching in rigid lines.
  * e.   all of the above.

4.   According to Leavitt (Cargo Beliefs and Religious Experience), older anthropological theories used to explain cargo cults cannot fully explain current cargo beliefs because
     a.   they were based on misunderstandings of native culture.
     b.   they failed to understand the power of Christianity in the lives of New Guinea peoples.
  * c.   they can't explain why cargo beliefs continue now that people in New Guinea know where cargo really comes from.
     d.   the acquisition of cargo did not improve people's lives.
     e.   people came to reject the materialism associated with cargo.

5. According to Leavitt, in 1971 a Bumbita leader named Yaliwan claimed that cargo would appear if people
   a. converted to Christianity and prayed for several hours each week.
   b. tore down their traditionally built houses and reconstructed their villages along Western lines.
   c. built an airstrip so that planes could land bearing their ancestors and Western goods.
 * d. removed cement survey markers from the top of a well-known nearby mountain.
   e. ceased to engage in extra marital affairs.

6.. Leavitt (Cargo Beliefs and Religious Experience) notes that anthropologists have identified four characteristics usually associated with revitalization movements. Which one is **not** mentioned as such a characteristic?
   a. response to colonial rule
   b. emphasis on ritual
   c. prophetic visions
 * d. return to original religious beliefs
   e. world transformation

7. According to Leavitt, an older Bumbita man named John believed
 * a. that a missionary who once gave him some salt was really the reincarnation of his father with whom he had once had a disagreement.
   b. that if two cement survey markers were removed from a well-known nearby mountain top, cargo would flow form it in abundance.
   c. God would give cargo if people converted to Christianity and prayed regularly.
   d. that gifts from God seen in dreams were really gifts from his grandfather, who had supported him when he was young.
   e. none of the above.

8. Leavitt (Cargo Beliefs and Religious Experience) feels that cargo beliefs persist among the Bumbita despite the fact that they now know where Western good come from, because
   a. they view cargo as a way to free themselves of government control.
   b. they know where cargo comes from but still can't get it.
 * c. they view cargo as a sign of support or forgiveness from their dead parents or grandparents.
   d. two of the above.
   e. a, b, and c above.

9. Leavitt (Cargo Beliefs and Religious Experience) reports that other anthropologists have explained the special emphasis on ancestors and the acquisition of western goods that characterize New Guinea cargo cults as a result of the fact that
    a. a large number of older people were killed by colonial administrations as they "pacified" New Guinea.
    b. dead close relatives were traditionally believed to be sources of support for their living descendants.
    c. goods played a large part through exchange in establishing relationships and gaining prestige in New Guinea society.
 * d. two of the above.
    e. a, b, and c above.

PART 9

CULTURE CHANGE AND APPLIED ANTHROPOLOGY

The introduction to Part 9 includes a discussion of basic concepts, such as innovation and acculturation, associated with culture change and applied anthropology.

KEY DEFINITIONS

Innovation is the invention of qualitatively new forms. It involves the recombination of what people already know into something different.

Borrowing refers to the adoption of something new from another group.

Diffusion is another word for borrowing often used by anthropologists who trace how an innovation is borrowed from one group to another.

Social acceptance is a process that inventions must pass through to become known and accepted by a group of people.

Cultural contact refers to the meeting of two culturally distinct groups.

Acculturation is the process of change that occurs due to cultural contact.

Applied anthropology includes any use of anthropological knowledge to influence social interaction, to maintain or change social institutions, or to direct the course of cultural change.

Adjustment anthropology uses anthropological knowledge to make interaction more predictable between people who use different cultural codes.

Administrative anthropology uses anthropological knowledge for planned change by those who are external to the local cultural group.

Action anthropology uses anthropological knowledge for planned change by the local group.

Advocate anthropology is the use of anthropological knowledge by the anthropologist to increase the power of self determination of the local group.

QUESTIONS

True or False?

T   1.   Innovation is the recombination of concepts, which are previously known, to form something qualitatively new.

F   2.   Acculturation refers to the process of learning one's culture.

F   3.   Social acceptance of an innovation involves three steps: identification, analysis, and substitution.

T   4.   If an anthropologist studied how the use of tobacco spread throughout the world, he or she would be interested in cultural diffusion.

T   5.   An anthropologist attempts to influence the way people treat tramps by publishing a book on tramp culture, thus making tramps more predictable to those who must deal with them. Such an anthropologist would be doing adjustment anthropology.

F   6.   Applied anthropology focuses on the use of anthropological knowledge to inform, enlighten, or increase the understanding of some individual or group.

T   7.   Action anthropology requires that the group which is to change has some legitimate process for making decisions.

F   8.   When an anthropologists attempts to make social interaction more predictable in cases where two people are operating with different cultural codes, he or she is doing action anthropology.

Multiple Choice

1.   A recombination of things that are known into something different is called
     a.   culture change.
 * b.   innovation.
     c.   social integration.
     d.   diffusion.
     e.   acculturation.

2.   An innovation is more likely to be accepted if it
     a.   meets a felt need.
     b.   meets needs for prestige.
     c.   maintains some continuity with traditional customs.
     d.   two of the above.
 * e.   a, b, and c above.

3. The process of change due to culture contact is called
   a. diffusion.
   b. borrowing.
   * c. acculturation.
   d. enculturation.
   e. revitalization.

4. Which of the following authors is an extreme diffusionist?
   * a. Erik von Däniken
   b. W. Lloyd Warner
   c. Emile Durkheim
   d. two of the above
   e. a, b, and c above

5. Any use of anthropological knowledge that makes social interaction more predictable among persons who operate with different cultural codes is called
   a. academic anthropology.
   b. action anthropology.
   c. administrative anthropology.
   * d. adjustment anthropology.
   e. advocate anthropology.

6. Any use of anthropological knowledge to influence social interaction, to maintain or change social institutions, or to direct the course of cultural change is called
   * a. applied anthropology.
   b. adjustment anthropology.
   c. advocate anthropology.
   d. administrative anthropology.
   e. academic anthropology.

7. In action anthropology, _____ initiate(s), control(s), and implement(s) planned change.
   a. administrators
   * b. the people affected by change
   c. the anthropologist
   d. two of the above
   e. a, b, and c above

8. Any use of anthropological knowledge by anthropologists to increase the power of self-determination of a particular cultural group is called
   a. action anthropology.
   b. academic anthropology.
   * c. advocate anthropology.
   d. adjustment anthropology.
   e. administrative anthropology.

Article 36

The Kayapo Resistance   TERENCE TURNER

Summary Over past two decades, there has been growing opposition to the cutting of the world's remaining old-growth forests and to the destruction of tribal peoples who live in them. For years it has been assumed that only powerful outsiders can save threatened environments and their inhabitants, not the threatened people themselves. A different perspective is presented by Terence Turner in this article about the Kayapo. Far from being wards of the world, these Indians have resisted the destruction of their Amazon forest and way of life with remarkable political sophistication.

The Kayapo are a Ge-speaking people living in the middle and lower Xingu River Valley in Brazil. They subsist using a combination of slash and burn agricultural and foraging. Although forest territory is vast compared to their population, they exploit most of their land each year for food by trekking to collect wild foods. Unlike Western environmentalists, Kayapo do not see the environment as a separate thing. Rather, it, along with the production of food and of children, is all part of one system. Thus, for them the destruction of the forest is equivalent to the destruction of their very being. The Kayapo have no special reverence for trees or forest animals. These are simply part of the single natural and social world they inhabit and use.

Over the past 30 years, the threat to Kayapo existence has grown enormous. There are encroaching settlers bent on cutting and farming the forest. There is a government-cut road through their preserve, isolating two villages from the rest. There have been illegal sales of Kayapo land and timber rights by some chiefs. Gold has been discovered and illegal mines employing thousands opened. There has been a plan to dump radioactive waste on the reservation.

The Kayapo have had few resources to fight these threats. Only a few speak Portuguese. Even fewer can read or use arithmetic. Yet early they used their meager assets to fight against the destruction of their lands. The two western communities cut off by the road banded together and killed over 50 Brazilians who had settled on their land. Other Kayapo attacked and captured the two gold mines, and by blockading the associated airstrip, managed to acquire rights to a portion of mining profits and the demarcation of more definite borders for their reservation. With their first share of the mining profits, they bought an airplane and hired a Brazilian pilot. They used the plane to patrol their territory, spotting squatters who were then killed or driven off by Indian patrols. They also set up bank accounts and a tribal office in Belem. Although there are still internal arguments over timber and land rights, and although there is also the beginning of a new class of wealthy natives, there is a sense of unity among Kayapo villages about defending against outside exploitation.

A key event occurred in 1989. The Kayapo had learned that the Brazilian government planned a series of dams that would flood much of their territory. The government would not reveal these plans in detail. To make the issue clear, the Kayapo planned an Indian congress in Altamira, a small town where one of the dams would be built. Kayapo leaders put together a coalition of over 40 different Indian nations, traveled to several countries including the United States, formed a coalition with environmentalist and human rights groups, invited the world press, and organized the event to avoid

141

violence. The event was a world media success and the Brazilian government delayed its dam-building plans.

Most remarkable about the incident was the ability of a small group of indigenous people to use the world communications system, to unite a variety of environmental and human rights groups that had previously often been at odds with one another, and to flawlessly organize an event in defense of their interests.

QUESTIONS

True or False?

T   1.   Turner (The Kayapo Resistence) notes that the Kayapo of Brazil, despite the small size of their mostly illiterate population, managed to gain control of two gold mines, buy an airplane, drive off or kill Brazilian settlers, stop the building of dams that would have flooded their land, unite many of the world's environmentalist and human rights groups, and receive a message of support from the Pope.

F   2.   According to Turner (The Kayapo Resistence), the forest and cultural existence of the Kayapo Indians of Brazil was preserved by the timely action of a variety of international environmental and human rights groups.

T   3.   Turner (The Kayapo Resistence) notes that despite occupying a large territory, the Kayapo Indians living along the Xingu River in Brazil use most of their territory when various sub groups make treks in it to collect wild foods.

F   4.   According to Turner, the Kayapo prevented the building of dams that would have flooded their lands by attacking, and if necessary, killing surveyors and construction workers.

T   5.   According to Turner, in 1989 the Kayapo Indians of Brazil staged an Indian Congress in Altamira, the site of a proposed dam that would have flooded some of their land, and in so doing managed to unite a number of international environmentalist and human rights groups in their cause.

F   6.   According to Turner, the rock star, Sting, representing his Indian land rights group, managed to unite over 40 Indian groups to attend a congress protesting plans by the Brazilian government to build a dam at a place called Altamira.

T   7.   Turner (The Kayapo Resistence) notes that because of concerted actions over a number of years, the Kayapo of Brazil managed to expand the lands that had been allotted to them to an area the size of Britain.

Multiple Choice

1. According to Turner (The Kayapo Resistance), a key to the success of the Kayapo in the preservation of their forest and way of life is
   a. the intervention of friendly legislators in the Brazilian parliament.
   * b. their ability to use the international media to mobilize world opinion.
   c. the help of world bank officials who were disturbed by the destructive impact of dam building.
   d. the use of money collected from gold mine profits to purchase land and prevent its settlement by outsiders.
   e. the help of rock star, Sting, and his native lands foundation.

2. Turner (The Kayapo Resistance) notes that the Kayapo of Brazil subsist by
   a. conducting slash and burn agriculture to grow such crops as maize, manioc, and yams.
   b. collecting wild foods, often using smaller groups who take treks in the forest.
   c. producing forest products for sale to nearby settlers.
   * d. two of the above.
   e. a, b, and c above.

3. According to Turner (The Kayapo Resistance), the Kayapo think of the forest as
   * a. part of a harmonious system that supplies natural energy to Kayapo natural and human production.
   b. a separate but essential part of their economic base.
   c. a fragile resources whose plants and animals must be protected with a special reverence.
   d. two of the above.
   e. a, b, and c above.

4. According to Turner, the lower and middle valley of the Xingu River where the Kayapo live is under attack in four of the following ways. Which one of the following is **not** a source of forest destruction?
   a. the encroachment of Brazilian settlers
   b. the discovery of gold on Kayapo lands
   * c. the discovery of oil on Kayapo lands
   d. the clear cutting of the region's forest by timber companies
   e. the building of dams

5. Turner notes that one of the great achievements of Payakan and other Kayapo Indian leaders was their ability to
   a. get rock star, Sting, to pay for their movement against the Brazilian government.
   * b. unite environmental groups, which had often been competitors, to back the Kayapo resistance against the building of a dam.
   c. to establish a forest products processing plant within the boundaries of their land that was completely Kayapo owned.
   d. two of the above.
   e. none of the above.

6. Four of the following are ways that the Kayapo Indians of Brazil have sought to prevent the destruction of their forest and way of life. Which one is **not**?
    a. a trip to Brazilia where, dressed in their feathers and war paint, they demonstrated against a proposal to dump nuclear wastes on their land
    b. a visit by leaders to a conference on tropical forest ecology held in the United States.
    c. the killing of 50 Brazilian squatters who had moved onto their land to farm and raise cattle
    d. the capture of two gold mines illegally located on Kayapo land
  * e. the formation of a forest cooperative with government sanctioned rights as sole owner of the land

Article 37

Medical Anthropology: Improving Nutrition in Malawi   SONIA PATTEN

Summary Patten's article does several things: it defines medical anthropology and illustrates one of its parts, applied medical anthropology; it describes a medical problem in another country (Malawi) and the USAID program that was designed to deal with it; and it reveals how an anthropologist contributes to program design and implementation and works with technically trained team members and local contacts.

Patten begins the article with a description of Malawi, a small, poor, dependent (on IMF and World Bank funds) Rift Valley country whose people subsist on corn (maize) and often go hungry. The project she worked on was designed to deal with a persistent problem, the malnutrition of children between the ages of about 3 and 5 and the 25 percent death rate caused by their enhanced susceptibility to disease. Funded by the U. S. Agency for International Development (USAID), it involved U.S. faculty members from the fields of nutrition, extension, animal science, veterinary medicine, crop science, and anthropology. Participants came from two U.S. universities and the University of Malawi.

Medical anthropology is the study of human health in a variety of cultural and environmental contexts. It consists of three main activities: the study of cultural differences in health beliefs and systems of healing, biomedical studies of human adaptations to disease, and applied medical anthropology. Patten participated as the medical anthropologist on the team chosen to work in Malawi. Her contribution involved the cultural side of the project. The team decided that the best way to provide protein to young children was by introducing goats that gave high milk yields. The animal science members of the team began a cross-breeding program to produce suitable milk goats that could survive in Malawi. Such programs, however, must be tailored to local cultural conditions. As the anthropologist, Patten designed a cultural baseline survey. She discovered that the local Chewa villagers were matrilineal and that men normally owned goats that they sold for meat. She helped to choose demonstration villages, organize meetings with women to gain their precipitation in the program, get the men to agree that milk goats would be owned by women and not sold for meat, and launch and design the goat distribution plan so that women would know how to handle goats and milk and repay the program with kids produced by their goats. In this way the program could be self-sufficient. She also helped with the medical evaluation program, which would necessitate the measurement and weighing of young children once a week. Despite goat theft problems (Malawi women solved this by keeping their goats close at hand) the program was a success and served as a model of similar programs in other parts of Malawi.

Patten concludes by noting the importance of anthropology, not only for the design and implementation of programs like this but also to help translate the local culture to U.S. team members who are not trained to discover it.

QUESTIONS

True or False?

F   1.   According to Patten (Improving Nutrition in Malawi), most medical anthropologists also have medical degrees.

T   2.   Patten (Improving Nutrition in Malawi) argues that there are at least three parts of medical anthropology: the study of health beliefs, the study of human adaptations to disease, and applied medical anthropology.

F   3.   According to Patten (Improving Nutrition in Malawi), the malnutrition of young children in Malawi was largely due to the fact that Chewa men owned and controlled the distribution of goats.

T   4.   According to Patten (Improving Nutrition in Malawi), an important problem with the introduction of milk goats into demonstration villages was theft of the goats.

F   5.   According to Patten (Improving Nutrition in Malawi), a persistent problem encountered by the program to introduce milk goats into demonstration villages was the unwillingness of men to allow women to own and keep goats.

T   6.   According to Patten (Improving Nutrition in Malawi), experiments with breeding goats for high milk yields and survivability showed that a cross between Saanen and local Malawi goats worked best.

F   7.   According to Patten (Improving Nutrition in Malawi), a major hurdle that had to be cleared when team members attempted to introduce milk goats into demonstration villages in Malawi was the persistent unwillingness of women to permit their children to be weighed and measured every week.

T   8.   According to Patten (Improving Nutrition in Malawi), Chewa women in demonstration villages asked members of the team supplying milk goats if they could teach them how to grow soy beans for an alternate supply of protein.

Multiple Choice

1.   According to Patten (Improving Nutrition in Malawi), there are several major fields within medical anthropology? Which one of the following is **not** such a field.
    a.   applied medical anthropology.
 * b.   cross-cultural medical ethics.
    c.   biomedical studies of human adaptations to disease.
    d.   the study of the differences in health beliefs and systems of healing.
    e.   none of the above.

146

2. According to Patten (Improving Nutrition in Malawi), Chewa babies, ages 1 to 2 or 3
   * a. show few signs of malnutrition.
   b. show signs of severe protein deficiency.
   c. are consistently short for their age.
   d. are underweight for their age.
   e. three of the above.

3. According to Patten (Improving Nutrition in Malawi), the USAID supported team of which she was a member decided to eliminate one community as a demonstration village because
   a. men would not allow women to own goats there.
   b. the land was not suitable for raising goats.
   * c. there was a serious goat theft problem there.
   d. it was a matrilineal rather than a patrilineal village.
   e. none of the above.

4. According to Patten (Improving Nutrition in Malawi), members of the USAID-sponsored applied program produced suitable milk goats by cross-breeding
   a. Saanen goats with Damascus goats.
   b. Malawi goats with Damascus goats.
   c. Anglo Nubian goats with Saanen goats.
   * d. Malawi goats with Saanen goats.
   e. Anglo Nubian goats with Malawi goats.

5. According to Patten (Improving Nutrition in Malawi), the first village activity she designed was a
   a. milk goat care demonstration.
   b. milk handling demonstration.
   c. child measurement and weighing survey.
   d. matrilineal descent social impact survey.
   * e. cultural baseline survey.

6. According to Patten (Improving Nutrition in Malawi), the staple food that makes up the bulk of the diet in Malawi is
   * a. corn (maize).
   b. sorgum.
   c. wheat.
   d. barley.
   e. rice.

7. According to Patten (Improving Nutrition in Malawi), the Chewa people of Malawi follow rules of
   a. patrilineal descent and matrilocal residence.
   b. patrilineal descent and patrilocal residence.
   * c. matrilineal descent and matrilocal residence.
   d. matrilineal descent and patrilocal residence.
   e. patrilineal descent and neolocal residence.

Article 38

Using Anthropology

DAVID W. McCURDY

Summary In this article, McCurdy discusses some of the professional applications of anthropology and argues that an anthropological perspective, characterized by ethnographic research, the concept of microculture, and cross-cultural sensitivity, can help anyone cope better with the everyday world.

He illustrates the argument using the case of a manager who is called upon to improve service to customer outlets operated by a large corporation. By using ethnographic research techniques when she assumes her new position, the manager discovers the detailed nature of the problem. The educational materials handled by the warehouse she must manage reach customer outlets in poor condition and improper amounts. Warehouse employees, who are under pressure to work rapidly, estimate rather than count the materials they ship to outlets. Books and other materials often arrive at outlets in a damaged condition. By shrink-wrapping books and reducing the size of shipping boxes, the manager speeds up work at the warehouse, assures that the right number of books and other materials are shipped, and improves the condition of the goods at their destination. By using an ethnographic or qualitative approach, she reveals the problem and makes it possible to find a realistic solution.

QUESTIONS

True or False?

F   1.   According to McCurdy, ethnographers work largely by administering and analyzing questionnaires.

T   2.   As he describes it in his article on the uses of anthropology, McCurdy notes that one of the problems at UTC was that warehouse workers failed to count books correctly.

F   3.   One disadvantage of using the ethnographic approach in management is that workers come to feel that no one cares about them.

T   4.   According to McCurdy, over half the PhDs in anthropology each year find employment outside of academia.

F   5.   McCurdy reports that an anthropologist who works as a consultant discovered that Chicago area natural gas consumers lied on questionnaires when they said they were trying to conserve energy.

Multiple Choice

1. According to McCurdy (Using Anthropology), the first thing a new manager at UTC did after assuming a new position was to
   a. shrink-wrap books in the warehouse.
   * b. ask warehouse workers, customer outlet staff, and other employees about problems and procedures.
   c. ask previous warehouse managers for advice.
   d. change the counting and shipping procedures in the warehouse.
   e. devise a new set of incentives to improve work output.

2. McCurdy (Using Anthropology) argues that _____ is an important skill that people who study anthropology can take into daily life.
   * a. ethnography
   b. knowledge of particular cultures
   c. the ability to conduct survey research
   d. knowledge of cross-cultural economics
   e. ethnology

3. Four of the following are problems experienced by customer outlet staff according to McCurdy (Using Anthropology). Which one is not?
   a. incorrect amounts of materials arriving at customer outlets
   b. frayed and worn books and other damaged materials
   * c. wrong materials sent by the central warehouse
   d. late deliveries of materials from the warehouse
   e. incorrect inventory

4. McCurdy claims that in many companies, newly installed managers tend to
   a. listen to their employees' suggestions.
   b. ask employees to teach them the new job.
   c. leave their employees alone.
   * d. impose a new agenda on their employees.
   e. none of the above.

5. According to McCurdy, an anthropologist was hired to find out why customers of a utility company failed to reduce energy consumption despite their claims that they were trying to conserve. He discovered that
   a. customers were lying.
   b. thermostats were faulty.
   c. meters were faulty.
   d. house insulation was usually insufficient.
   * e. fathers turned down thermostats, other family members turned them up.

Article 39

Career Advice for Anthropology Undergraduates   JOHN T. OMOHUNDRO

Summary In this article, John Omohundro observes the anxiety felt by anthropology majors about their employability and describes a course of action students can follow to find work. At the root of the problem is the inability of BA graduates to know about or connect with a world of work that has been a mystery to them during their school years. The result is a six month to a year delay in finding employment after graduation. To speed up the transition from college to work, graduates need to learn how to identify and translate the skills they learned as anthropology majors into appropriate résumé language.

Omohundro also points out that many anthropology professors hesitate to advise their students about careers because they feel they don't know enough about today's careers, or why and how people change careers so often these days, and because they have an aversion to "vocationalism."

To find a career quickly, Omohundro suggests using two skills associated with anthropology—ethnographic discovery and translation. Students must recall what their anthropological experiences are, identify the skills associated with these experiences, discover what skills employers are looking for, and learn to translate their anthropological skills into words employers can understand by mastering résumé language. Omohundro includes tables listing some anthropological skills and phrases that can be used in résumé language to describe them. He notes that this language should have a high degree of *indexicality* or meaningfulness to its intended audience. He labels the whole process of presenting oneself in the job market *trans-cultural self-presentation*.

The final section of the article presents evidence from surveys that indicates that a large majority of anthropology majors find work related to their discipline and that three quarters of them feel that anthropology helps them at work.

QUESTIONS

True or False?

T   1.   According to Omohundro (Career Advice), anthropology majors have a difficult time knowing how to apply for a job because they live in a society where there are an enormous number of different jobs and where their lives have been separated from the world of work during childhood.

F   2.   According to Omohundro (Career Advice), it is difficult to translate the skills learned as an anthropology major into those required in the world of work because anthropology is such a different and esoteric discipline.

T   3.   Omohundro (Career Advice) points out that many professors hesitate to give their students career advice because they don't believe they know enough about careers, because people change careers often these days, and because many of them have a prejudice against vocationalism.

F   4.   According to Omohundro (Career Advice), students approach the job market with over-confidence because they are ignorant of what the real requirements of getting a job are.

T   5.   In his article "Career Advice for Anthropology Undergraduates," Omonundro describe the process of translating his students' anthropology skills into language employers can understand as "trans-cultural self-presentation."

F   6.   Omohundro (Career Advice), argues that it is difficult to translate anthropological skill into terms that employers can understand, so anthropology students may have to invent some experiences that will impress job interviewers.

T   7.   Citing survey evidence, Omohundro (Career Advice) notes that over 70 percent of the graduates polled thought that anthropology was useful to them at work and that 74 percent were glad they had majored in the subject.

Multiple Choice

1.   According to Omohundro (Career Advice for Undergraduate Anthropologists), anthropology BAs can speed up the process of finding a job after graduation by
     a.   taking remedial computer courses following graduation.
     b.   telling prospective employers the kinds of anthropological experiences they have had.
 *   c.   learning to identify their anthropological skills, the skills employers need, and the résumé language necessary to communicate the skills to employers.
     d.   learning some of the basic ways to present themselves at interviews, such as how to dress, how to sit, how to talk, and how to show interest.
     e.   learning to be more humble and less self aggrandizing.

2.   According to Omohundro (Career Advice), the process of connecting one's anthropological skills with skills employers are looking for is called
     a.   indexicality.
     b.   anthro-shock.
 *   c.   trans-cultural self-presentation.
     d.   ethnographic translation.
     e.   network participatory presentation.

3. According to Omohundro (Career Advice), many anthropology professors hesitate to give career advice because they
   a. don't believe they know enough about the world of work.
   b. do not believe anthropology is useful for anything.
   c. have an aversion to "vocationalism."
   * d. two of the above.
   e. a, b, and c above.

4. Omonundro (Career Advice) notes that James Spradley observed that
   a. young people in simpler societies often feel anxiety about the transition to the adult world of work.
   b. young people in simpler societies do not need to learn work skills because work is not complex in such groups.
   * c. young people in complex societies have a difficult time knowing how to chose and obtain a job.
   d. young people in any society find it difficult to move into a career.
   e. none of the above.

5. According to Omohundro (Careers Advice), it takes the average undergraduate BA year(s) after graduation to find employment.
   a. two
   b. three
   c. two and one-half
   * d. one-half to one
   e. one and one-half

6. According to Omohundro (Career Advice), which of the following are skills anthropology BAs will find useful in the world of work?
   a. using statistics.
   b. interviewing.
   c. analyzing craft techniques.
   d. two of the above.
   * e. a, b, and c above.

NOTES

NOTES

NOTES

NOTES